by Charlie Josephine

SAMUEL FRENCH

ISBN 978-0-573-00041-6

concordtheatricals.co.uk
concordtheatricals.com

FOR AMATEUR PRODUCTION ENQUIRIES

UNITED KINGDOM AND WORLD
EXCLUDING NORTH AMERICA
licensing@concordtheatricals.co.uk
020-7054-7298

Each title is subject to availability from Concord Theatricals, depending upon country of performance.

This work is published by Samuel French, an imprint of Concord Theatricals Ltd.

Professional rights in this title are controlled by The Agency (London) Ltd, 24 Pottery Lane, London W11 4LN.

USE OF COPYRIGHTED MUSIC

A licence issued by Concord Theatricals to perform this play does not include permission to use the incidental music specified in this publication. In the United Kingdom: Where the place of performance is already licensed by the PERFORMING RIGHT SOCIETY (PRS) a return of the music used must be made to them. If the place of performance is not so licensed then application should be made to PRS for Music (www.prsformusic.com). A separate and additional licence from PHONOGRAPHIC PERFORMANCE LTD (www.ppluk.com) may be needed whenever commercial recordings are used. Outside the United Kingdom: Please contact the appropriate music licensing authority in your territory for the rights to any incidental music.

USE OF COPYRIGHTED THIRD-PARTY MATERIALS

Licensees are solely responsible for obtaining formal written permission from copyright owners to use copyrighted third-party materials (e.g., artworks, logos) in the performance of this play and are strongly cautioned to do so. If no such permission is obtained by the licensee, then the licensee must use only original materials that the licensee owns and controls. Licensees are solely responsible and liable for clearances of all third-party copyrighted materials, and shall indemnify the copyright owners of the play(s) and their licensing agent, Concord Theatricals Ltd., against any costs, expenses, losses and liabilities arising from the use of such copyrighted third-party materials by licensees.

IMPORTANT BILLING AND CREDIT REQUIREMENTS

If you have obtained performance rights to this title, please refer to your licensing agreement for important billing and credit requirements.

ABOUT THE ROYAL SHAKESPEARE COMPANY

The Shakespeare Memorial Theatre was founded by Charles Flower, a local brewer, and opened in Stratford-upon-Avon in 1879. Since then, the plays of Shakespeare have been performed here, alongside the work of his contemporaries and of current contemporary playwrights. In 1960, the Royal Shakespeare Company as we now know it was formed by Peter Hall and Fordham Flower. The founding principles were threefold: the Company would embrace the freedom and power of Shakespeare's work, train and develop young actors and directors and, crucially, experiment in new ways of making theatre. The RSC quickly became known for exhilarating performances of Shakespeare alongside new masterpieces such as *The Homecoming* and *Old Times* by Harold Pinter. It was a combination that thrilled audiences, and this close and exacting relationship between writers from different eras has become the fuel that powers the creativity of the RSC.

In 1974, The Other Place opened in a tin hut on Waterside under the visionary leadership and artistic directorship of Buzz Goodbody. Determined to explore Shakespeare's plays in intimate proximity to her audience and to make small-scale, radical new work, Buzz revitalised the Company's interrogation of the relationship between the contemporary and classical repertoire. This was followed by the founding of the Swan Theatre in 1986 – a space dedicated to Shakespeare's contemporaries, as well as later plays from the Restoration period, alongside living writers.

In nearly 60 years of producing new plays, we have collaborated with some of the most exciting writers of their generation. These have included: Edward Albee, Howard Barker, Alice Birch, Richard Bean, Edward Bond, Howard Brenton, Marina Carr, Lolita Chakrabarti, Caryl Churchill, Martin Crimp, Can Dündar, David Edgar, Helen Edmundson, James Fenton, Georgia Fitch, Robin French, Juliet Gilkes Romero, Fraser Grace, David Greig, Tanika Gupta, Matt Hartley, Ella Hickson, Kirsty Housley, Dennis Kelly, Hannah Khalil, Anders Lustgarten, Tarell Alvin McCraney, Martin McDonagh, Tom Morton-Smith, Rona Munro, Richard Nelson, Anthony Neilson, Harold Pinter, Phil Porter, Mike Poulton, Mark Ravenhill, Somalia Seaton, Adriano Shaplin, Tom Stoppard, debbie tucker green, Frances Ya-Chu Cowhig, Timberlake Wertenbaker, Peter Whelan and Roy Williams.

The RSC is committed to illuminating the relevance of Shakespeare's plays and the works of his contemporaries for the next generation of audiences and believes that our continued investment in new plays and living writers is a central part of that mission.

The work of the RSC is supported by the Culture Recovery Fund

Miranda Curtis CMG - Lead Production Supporter of *Cowbois*

New Work at the RSC is generously supported by The Drue and H.J. Heinz II Charitable Trust

The RSC Acting Companies are generously supported by The Gatsby Charitable Foundation

NEW WORK AT THE RSC

We are a contemporary theatre company built on classical rigour. Through an extensive programme of research and development, we support writers, directors and actors to explore and develop new ideas for our stages, and as part of this we commission playwrights to engage with the muscularity and ambition of the classics and to set Shakespeare's world in the context of our own.

We invite writers to spend time with us in our rehearsal rooms, with our actors and creative teams. Alongside developing new plays for all our stages, we invite playwrights to contribute dramaturgically to both our productions of Shakespeare and his contemporaries, as well as our work for, and with, young people. We believe that engaging with living writers and contemporary theatre-makers helps to establish a creative culture within the Company which both inspires new work and creates an ever more urgent sense of enquiry into the classics.

Shakespeare was a great innovator and breaker of rules, as well as a bold commentator on the times in which he lived. It is his spirit which informs new work at the RSC.

Support us and make a difference; for more information visit **www.rsc.org.uk/support**

This production of *Cowbois* was first performed by the Royal Shakespeare Company in the Swan Theatre, Stratford-upon-Avon, on 14 October 2023. The cast was as follows:

BRIDGETTE AMOFAH (she/her)	**MARY**
LEE BRAITHWAITE (they/he)	**LUCY/LOU**
SHAUN DINGWALL (he/him)	**FRANK/TOMMY**
MICHAEL ELCOCK (he/him)	**GEORGE**
COLM GORMLEY (he/him)	**JOHN**
VINNIE HEAVEN (they/them)	**JACK**
PAUL HUNTER (he/him)	**SHERIFF ROGER JONES**
LUCY McCORMICK (she/her)	**JAYNE**
SOPHIE MELVILLE (she/her)	**MISS LILLIAN**
JULIAN MOORE-COOK (he/him)	**JAMES**
EMMA PALLANT (she/her)	**SALLY-ANN**
LJ PARKINSON (they/them)	**CHARLEY PARKHURST**
ROBERT ADDI	**KID**
AIDEN COLE	**KID**
ALASTAIR NGWENYA	**KID**

All other parts played and understudied by members of the Company.

CREATIVE TEAM

WRITER	**CHARLIE JOSEPHINE (they/he)**
CO-DIRECTORS	**CHARLIE JOSEPHINE (they/he)**
	SEAN HOLMES (he/him)
DESIGNER	**GRACE SMART (she/her)**
LIGHTING	**SIMEON MILLER (he/him)**
MUSIC	**JIM FORTUNE (he/him)**
SOUND AND SOUNDSCAPE	**MWEN**
MOVEMENT	**JENNIFER JACKSON (she/her)**
FIGHTS AND INTIMACY	**BETHAN CLARK (she/her)**
DRAMATURG	**REBECCA LATHAM (she/her)**
MUSIC DIRECTOR	**GEMMA STORR (she/them)**
VOICE AND TEXT	**GARY HORNER (he/him)**
DRAMATHERAPIST	**WABRIYA KING (she/her)**
ASSISTANT DIRECTOR	**PRIME ISAAC (she/her)**
CASTING DIRECTOR	**MARTIN POILE (he/him)**
CHILDREN'S CASTING DIRECTOR	**CHARLIE METCALF (she/her)**
HEAD OF NEW WORK	**PIPPA HILL (she/her)**
PRODUCTION MANAGERS	**MARK GRAHAM (he/him)**
	KURT MOORES (he/him)
COSTUME SUPERVISOR	**SIAN HARRIS (she/her)**
COMPANY MANAGERS	**LINDA FITZPATRICK (she/her)**
	PIP HOROBIN (she/her)
	SUZY BOURKE (she/her)
STAGE MANAGER	**ROB WALKER (he/him)**
DEPUTY STAGE MANAGER	**CHERYL FIRTH (she/her)**
ASSISTANT STAGE MANAGER	**GRACE HANS (they/them)**
LEAD CHAPERONE	**DIANE FORD (she/her)**
PRODUCER	**BEN TYREMAN (he/him)**
PRODUCTION COORDINATOR	**JADE PARKIN (she/her)**

MUSICIANS

GUITAR	**YUE MIYAGI (she/her)**
BASS	**SARAH ROSE HIGGINS (she/her)**
DRUMS	**JOELLE BARKER (she/her)**

This text may differ slightly from the play as performed.

THE ROYAL SHAKESPEARE COMPANY

THANKS

Thank you to Erica Whyman and Pippa Hill for trusting me to write this. Thank you Becky Latham for your delicate dramaturgy. Simon Stephens for FaceTime chats over lockdown. Yasser Zadeh for your swagger. Duncan Macmillian for your 'big play' boost. My mum for everything. Thank you Kit Heyam, Jen Manion, Jack Halbertsam, Emily Skidmore, Adrienne Maree Brown and Susan Stryker for your work. Thank you Ben Tyreman for your queer activism in a straight venue. Thank you Jonathan for your consistent care and kindness. Thank you Sean Holmes, for believing in me, for being the best collaborator, and not a bad bloke. Thank you Jessica and Seahorse – I wrote this before I met you, which feels wild, like maybe it was a spell, somehow we made magic, thank you, I love you.

CHARACTERS

JACK – a nonbinary trans masc cowboy (they/he)

MISS LILLIAN – a white woman, who's husband owns the saloon (she/her)

SALLY ANN – a god-fearing white cis woman, who's husband is a miner (she/her)

MARY – a Black woman, a widow, mother of Kid, a farmer (she/her)

KID – a young boy with a touch of magic (he/him)

JAYNE – a school teacher, who's fiancé is a miner (she/her)

LUCY / LOU – a Black farmer, AFAB nonbinary trans masc (she/her, then later they/he)

SHERIFF ROGER JONES – a cis man, an alcoholic, a good gun (he/him)

FRANK – a white cis man, Lillian's husband, the saloon owner (he/him)

JOHN – a white cis man, a miner, Sally Ann's husband (he/him)

JAMES – a Latinx or Black cis man, a miner, Jayne's fiancé (he/him)

GEORGE – a Black cis man, a farmer, Lucy's husband (he/him)

CHARLEY PARKHURST – a nonbinary person, a famous bandit and gun fighter (they/them)

TOMMY – a cis man, a bandit (he/him)

TOMMY'S TOOTHLESS BOYS – a gang of bandits (he/him)

AUTHOR'S NOTES

Script Notes

Stage directions are in italics and brackets.

A / indicates a fast run onto the next line, almost an interruption.

A /.. indicates where a word can't be found and the character does something else to express themselves. It could be a small pedestrian gesture or an abstract movement.

A . indicates where a character should have a line but for some reason are choosing not to speak.

Casting Preferences

If the character is trans, the actor must be. If the character is queer, the actor must be. Unless their race is specifically stated in the description above the actor does not need to be white, and probably shouldn't be. Actors are encouraged to perform this play in their own accents, despite the 1880s American vocabulary and iconography.

ACT ONE

Defrosting

(It's 1883, Wild West, USA. But it's also 2023, Swan Theatre, SUA. The world of this play straddles both these two times and places.)

(Lights up on **MISS LILLIAN** *praying. Halfway through she fiddles with the underwire of her bra. Tries to be godly, sighs, frustrated. Finishes her prayers. Gets up and opens the shutters, and we see that she is in fact in the middle of a saloon. She sits down with her breakfast. There's a sharp rap at the door. She tries to ignore it. The knocking returns, is persistent. She reluctantly unlocks the door.* **SALLY ANN** *bursts in.)*

SALLY ANN. Good day to you Miss Lillian!

MISS LILLIAN. Good day to/

SALLY ANN. oh I'm so pleased I've caught you! So pleased it's true! For I come on a matter of the most urgency, oh I'm not disrupting your breakfast am I?

MISS LILLIAN. Well/

SALLY ANN. what are you having there? Grits is it? With sugar or salt?

MISS LILLIAN. What, erm neither/

SALLY ANN. neither?! What, *nothing* on them?!

MISS LILLIAN. No?

SALLY ANN. Oh my! That's very queer! *Nothing on them?!* I must say I *always* add a little salt to mine, you should try that, try a little salt. Not too much of course, all things in moderation as the Good Lord intended. But yes just a little, to bring out the flavour, a pinch is all you need, what *nothing* on them? Very queer! And *black* coffee is it? No milk?

MISS LILLIAN. No. No I/

SALLY ANN. ah! Well! Each man to himself as they say. And I guess each woman too. The Good Lord did indeed make us all different!

MISS LILLIAN. Indeed/

SALLY ANN. indeed, and loves us all! Each and every one! All things bright and beautiful! In truth I thought I'd be interrupting your morning devotion, if interrupting anything at all, I of course don't care to intrude on anyone's precious time with The Lord, you have committed your soul to the Good Lord for the day?

MISS LILLIAN. I've, prayed, yes/

SALLY ANN. praise be! I'm very glad to hear so! And happy I didn't intrude.

MISS LILLIAN. Not at all/

SALLY ANN. it's just I'm driven by some *urgent* business. Business of the most urgency.

MISS LILLIAN. Is it about the pastor?

SALLY ANN. Have you news?! Oh god saves us all! God save us/

MISS LILLIAN. no! No I've no news!

SALLY ANN. Oh. But we must *have* a pastor Miss Lillian!

MISS LILLIAN. I know, which is why/

SALLY ANN. we *must*!

MISS LILLIAN. I agree! And that's/

SALLY ANN. a strong voice of reason and pillar of support, especially, under the current circumstances.

MISS LILLIAN. Yes, and that's exactly why/

SALLY ANN. I am of course happy to play my part. To be a servant to the Good Lord is my only wish, my *only* wish! But I simply cannot be responsible for saving the souls of an entire town, I am but one woman after all! Limited! By my position! By my sex! By my intellectual capabilities, by my/

MISS LILLIAN. Sally Ann! No one is asking you to save any souls!

SALLY ANN. We *need* a pastor/

MISS LILLIAN. I know! And that's why I wrote to the Bishop in Georgetown. Wrote to Denver too. You were there when I wrote the letters, walked with me to the coach driver, watched him ride off with them in/

SALLY ANN. nearly *three* months ago!

MISS LILLIAN. What would you have me do? I can't *make* them reply any sooner than they're willing or able/

SALLY ANN. of course!

MISS LILLIAN. So then it is perhaps, as you say yourself, so often, an opportunity to practise patience.

SALLY ANN. I do say that, you're right... You know, it is of course above my station to even *think* it, but it's true I have often considered myself to have the capabilities of a great pastor. I believe I've been blessed with a great many talents that the position requires. Inspiring a crowd, for example, with a rousing/

(**JAYNE** *enters.*)

JAYNE. oh Miss Lillian!

MISS LILLIAN. Good morning Jayne.

SALLY ANN. Good day to you Jayne/

JAYNE. it is *not* a good day, nor a good morning, decidedly it is not!

SALLY ANN. Whatever is the matter?

JAYNE. Dammit the new school books I ordered *still* haven't arrived!

SALLY ANN. Neither has a reply from the bishop, if you can believe/

JAYNE. I can't bear to begin a new semester with the same books the children have read through *seven* times already! I just can't bear it, oh are you eating, are we disturbing you?

MISS LILLIAN. Well I/

JAYNE. grits is it? Sweet or savoury?

SALLY ANN. Neither! She has them *plain!*

JAYNE. *Plain* grits?! How queer!

SALLY ANN. Just as I exclaimed! The very same! It *is* queer Miss Lillian to eat them with neither sugar nor salt/

JAYNE. I've plenty spare, if you need/

MISS LILLIAN. I couldn't remember, what I liked since, not since. So I've had them plain and/

JAYNE. grief does funny things to you, it's true.

SALLY ANN. Grief? Why Jayne, nobody's died!

MISS LILLIAN. Sally Ann, I'm sure Jayne didn't/

SALLY ANN. they're missing! Not dead!

JAYNE. It's still a grief to bear though is it not? This endless waiting?!

SALLY ANN. Speaking of them as though they're dead/

JAYNE. I wasn't! I was merely expressing/

SALLY ANN. dead and buried in the ground? How heartless!

JAYNE. Heartless?!

MISS LILLIAN. Ladies!

JAYNE. I see my sweet fiancé out the corner of my eye. Swear I could feel him beside me. Then I think of them all, trapped underground, and my blood runs cold/

SALLY ANN. and yet you speak of them so carelessly?

JAYNE. You're the one who's careless/

SALLY ANN. how dare you/

MISS LILLIAN. ladies please! It's far too early for quarrelling! Our husbands *will* return. They will have found gold. Our town will be saved. Jayne, I'll send a note to the bookstore in Denver tomorrow morning. Sally Ann, if we haven't heard by Monday I'll send more letters. You may watch me write them, again, if you wish.

JAYNE. I'm sure she does.

SALLY ANN. Good day to you both.

*(***SALLY ANN** *storms out of the saloon. Bumping into* **LUCY** *as she goes.)*

LUCY. What's caught her skirt on fire?

MISS LILLIAN. Never you mind.

JAYNE. Could be anything in truth, they easily catch.

LUCY. That they do. Mornin' all.

MISS LILLIAN & JAYNE. Mornin'.

LUCY. It's gettin' hot out already. Breakfast is it?

MISS LILLIAN. Was, cold now I suppose/

LUCY. grits is it?

JAYNE. With nothing on them!

MISS LILLIAN. Oh for god's sake!

LUCY. Nothing? I salt *and* sugar mine/

JAYNE. both?

LUCY. Both! Half each, then stir 'em together.

JAYNE. You don't!

LUCY. I do! Been that way ever since a young 'un. Never tried it?

JAYNE. Can't say I have.

LUCY. Well you're missin' out Miss Jayne!

JAYNE. I doubt that.

MISS LILLIAN. What can I do for you Lucy?

LUCY. Came to share bad news/

JAYNE. oh great/

LUCY. 'bout old Duke.

JAYNE. Oh no!

LUCY. Yup!

MISS LILLIAN. Oh no! Well I'm mighty sorry Luce. I know he was your daddy's horse.

LUCY. Sure was.

JAYNE. Was a fine beast.

LUCY. That too.

MISS LILLIAN. How'd he die?

LUCY. I shot him.

MISS LILLIAN & JAYNE. What?!

LUCY. Found him this mornin'. Knew instantly somethin' weren't right. His leg was broke, the bone poking right through.

JAYNE. Ugh!

LUCY. Knew straight away what my George would do. Got the shotgun and/

JAYNE. oh my!

LUCY. Don't mind admitting it took a while to muster up within myself, the courage to pull the trigger but, praise be I managed it.

JAYNE. Praise be? Well I must say I'm shocked!

LUCY. At what?

JAYNE. You shooting a horse dead is what!

LUCY. It needed doin'!

JAYNE. But not by you! Why, don't you know you're a lady?!

(**LUCY** *squirms.*)

LUCY. Well, there ain't no men around!

JAYNE. Don't cha think I know that?

MISS LILLIAN. Ladies, let's not get too/

JAYNE. you think I've *forgotten?!*

LUCY. Well I don't know! It just seems a foolish thing to say/

JAYNE. oh so I'm a *fool* now too?!

MISS LILLIAN. Ladies!

LUCY. Seems to me that sometimes you gotta let go of being a lady to get things done.

MISS LILLIAN. We're just surprised is all.

LUCY. What would you have me do? *Wait,* for some *man,* to ride on through this god forsaken town that's barely on the map/

MISS LILLIAN. hey! That's not/

LUCY. for nothin' but the *joy* of it, cus Lord knows there'd be no other reason for visitin'! Wait for some man to shoot a dying horse that I could easily shoot myself except *I'm a lady* and lady's don't put poor beasts out their misery?

JAYNE. Hell! I still don't think I could shoot a horse! Makes my blood run cold to even consider it.

MISS LILLIAN. Me too!

LUCY. Well I did what I had to. No shame in that. If you want me to go I'll go/

MISS LILLIAN. of course not/

LUCY. just wanted a little company is all, maybe some coffee if you can spare some.

MISS LILLIAN. There's that there. I'll heat it for you.

LUCY. I'll have it cold, that's fine, you done with these grits too?

MISS LILLIAN. I/

LUCY. where's your salt?

MISS LILLIAN. I'll fetch it.

LUCY. And sugar?

MISS LILLIAN. That too.

*(**KID** bursts in shooting his wooden gun and jumping on the furniture.)*

KID. Bang bang bang!

MISS LILLIAN. Hey! Careful! Careful! Get down from there!

KID. Bang bang *bang!*

MISS LILLIAN. Please get down from there before you/

MARY. GET DOWN! *NOW!*

*(**KID** jumps down obediently. **MARY** enters.)*

KID. Sorry mama.

MARY. It's not my furniture you was jumping all over.

KID. Sorry Miss Lillian.

MISS LILLIAN. You're forgiven. But only cus you're so cute.

*(**MISS LILLIAN** kisses the top of **KID**'s head. He shrugs her off to go play. She watches him wistfully.)*

MARY. Where's Sally Ann at?

LUCY. Just missed her.

MARY. Ah! I miss her promising to pray for me. Best thing 'bout being a widow is you get all the patronising prayers.

*(**JAYNE** and **LUCY** don't know where to look.)*

Ah come on I'm joking! It's been well over a year now, and still no one joins me in a little jest.

JAYNE. Don't seem much jest about the dead.

MARY. There's plenty believe me. And I hope you don't find that out for yourself anytime soon.

JAYNE. .

MARY. Any coffee goin'?

MISS LILLIAN. I'll brew some.

LUCY. Don't forget the sugar Miss Lillian.

MISS LILLIAN. Yes of course.

LUCY. And the salt.

MARY. Can't you get your own sugar n salt?

LUCY. She offered!

MARY. Well she shouldn't have! Always looking after everyone else, bet she ain't even eaten.

LUCY. You have ain't ya Miss Lillian?

MARY. You eating her breakfast?!

LUCY. You're drinking her coffee!

MISS LILLIAN. Ladies!

MARY. You know we're on rations/

LUCY. I know!

MARY. So why you eating her/

LUCY. I thought she'd finished!

MISS LILLIAN. Ladies!

SHERIFF. Ladies ladies ladies! It's a *beautiful* morning!

(The **SHERIFF** *staggers in, drunk and thirsty.* **MISS LILLIAN** *stops him getting to the bar.* **MARY** *jumps up to free her seat.* **JAYNE** *and* **LUCY** *instantly move anything fragile down the other end of the table.)*

It's beautiful! Beautiful! *Beautiful!*

MARY. *(Sarcastic.)* Sure is.

*(***MISS LILLIAN** *glares at* **MARY**, *and smiles at the* **SHERIFF**.*)*

MISS LILLIAN. What can I do for ya Sheriff?

SHERIFF. There she is! Always thinking I want for somethin'?! When actually all a man's doing is passing by, checkin' up on the ladies, seeing if I can be of any assistance.

MISS LILLIAN. You know I can't serve you before lunchtime Sheriff/

SHERIFF. I know! I know!

MISS LILLIAN. It's the law!

SHERIFF. I know, I *know!* I *am* the law!

MARY. Could have fooled me.

SHERIFF. It's my leg you see. Old war wound. Back when I was defending this here territory against goddamn confederate sympathisers and/

MISS LILLIAN. Sheriff! No guns/

EVERYONE. no politics!

SHERIFF. We got ambushed! Dirty goddam bandits claiming the constitution was unlawful. Goddam dirty/

MISS LILLIAN. Sheriff/

SHERIFF. well we got into it all right! Told 'em they'd have to *vacate.* Looked 'em right in the eye and said *get!* Then their back-up-boys goddamn bushwhacked us, good and proper! Took a bullet here in the hip, right deep into the bone/

EVERYONE. right there in the joint socket.

SHERIFF. That's right! But I still managed to get up n shoot n kill/

EVERYONE. all three in front of me.

SHERIFF. The rest of our boys took care of the rest of 'em. Pow pow pow! Put 'em all down!

(He gets too close to **MARY***.)*

There was a time when I was quite the gun you know.

MARY. *(Unimpressed.)* That right?

SHERIFF. Quite the gun!

JAYNE. So what happened Sheriff?

SHERIFF. Well! The war ended and, this town dried up and. I guess I got thirsty!

(The **SHERIFF** *laughs loudly, no one else does.)*

How about it Lillian?

MISS LILLIAN. No! I can't!

SHERIFF. Just one for the road?

LUCY. Where's your salt at Lillian?

MISS LILLIAN. I'll fetch it/

KID. Mama? Play with me?

MARY. In a minute!

(The **SHERIFF** *sings* **["WHISKEY ON A SUNDAY"]** *by The Dubliners.* **KID** *bang bang bangs around the space.)*

LUCY. I can do it/

MISS LILLIAN. no, I'll get it, you sit/

MARY. she can get it herself! Sit down and have your breakfast!

(School bell rings.)

JAYNE. Oh gawd! Don't make me go please!

MISS LILLIAN. The children need you Jayne!

MARY. What's the matter?

JAYNE. I can't read those same books *again!*

LUCY. If you just tell me Lillian where the salt is/

MARY. why, ain't the new books arrived yet?

MISS LILLIAN. Just a moment/

JAYNE. no they ain't!

KID. Mama? Mama?!

MARY. Yes baby?

KID. Play with me?

MARY. Yes baby. I thought you ordered them Lillian?

MISS LILLIAN. yes! I did/

LUCY. I could get it myself/

MISS LILLIAN. just a moment. I'm, *Sheriff?!*

(The **SHERIFF** *has snuck behind the bar.)*

No! Sheriff no/

(She tries to grab the bottle from him and he pulls her into a hug.)

SHERIFF. Finest woman in town this one!

(The **SHERIFF** *tries dancing with her. He's heavy and she struggles to hold him up.)*

Finest woman in town!

MISS LILLIAN. OK let's get you seated there Sheriff.

*(***MISS LILLIAN** *helps the* **SHERIFF** *to his chair.)*

*(***MISS LILLIAN** *sighs relief.)*

*(***MISS LILLIAN** *turns to get the salt and* **KID** *is suddenly in her face with a wooden gun.)*

KID. Bang bang bang!

MISS LILLIAN. Woah! No guns in this saloon/

SHERIFF. stick 'em up kid!

MARY. No, no Sheriff he/

KID. bang bang bang! I *got* you Sheriff!

SHERIFF. That you did boy, got me shot *dead!*

MARY. Don't teach him that!

KID. Dead!

MARY. Oh marvellous!

KID. Shot him dead! Shot him dead!

SHERIFF. What? He needs to learn sooner or later/

MARY. don't tell me how to raise my son!

MISS LILLIAN. Mary/

KID. bang bang bang!

SHERIFF. I'm just sayin' the boy needs to/

MARY. I do *not* need child-raising lessons from *you* Sheriff!

(School bell rings. **JAYNE** *groans.)*

LUCY. There's the bell again.

JAYNE. Oh gawd don't make me!

SHERIFF. All I'm sayin' is/

MISS LILLIAN. Sheriff please/

SHERIFF. there's just some things a woman just can't teach a boy.

MARY. Ain't *nothing* a man can teach him that I can't!

SHERIFF. Like dancing! And shooting! And f/

(The **SHERIFF** *pulls his gun out of his belt and everyone panics. He tries to dance with the bottle and mime shooting his gun too.*

He stumbles, and **MISS LILLIAN** *somehow manages to get the gun off him. She puts it on the bar. The* **SHERIFF** *sits slumped on the floor, his back against the bar, suddenly upset.)*

MISS LILLIAN. There we go.

SHERIFF. I'm sorry!

MISS LILLIAN. I know/

SHERIFF. I'm sorry/

MISS LILLIAN. it's all right, you're all right.

(He nurses the bottle and half falls asleep. It's a sorry sight. The women are disgusted and sad. School bell rings.)

You best get over to that school yard Jayne.

JAYNE. But/

MISS LILLIAN. the children are waiting.

*(***JAYNE** *sulks away.)*

LUCY. I best be going too. Them fields ain't gonna plough themselves/

KID. bang bang bang/

LUCY. the earth's all baked in the sun/

KID. bang bang *bang!*

*(***LUCY** *mimes shooting* **KID** *and turns to exit.)*

MISS LILLIAN. Oh Lucy, take the Sheriff will you?

LUCY. Do I have to?

MARY. Yes! She asked ya didn't she/

LUCY. well alright/

MISS LILLIAN. please! There's a cot in his cell, he can sleep it off there.

LUCY. Come on then Sheriff.

(**LUCY** *half carries half drags the* **SHERIFF** *off.*)

MARY. Kid! Go play on the porch!

KID. Won't you play with me?

MARY. Not now.

KID. But mama/

MARY. but nothing! Go on now. And don't you stray off that porch, you hear me?

KID. Yes mama.

(**KID** *rides an invisible horse away.*)

MISS LILLIAN. I'm sorry about the Sheriff. He didn't mean anything by it, he just/

MARY. the man's drunk. Why you apologising for him?

MISS LILLIAN. Who else is gonna?

MARY. You don't gotta keep doing everything for everyone! It'll make you sick.

MISS LILLIAN. I know/

MARY. gotta learn to say no!

MISS LILLIAN. I know/

MARY. or they'll keep pushing for more and more.

MISS LILLIAN. I know! ... I love you Mary.

MARY. (*Whispers.*) Let's get out of here!

MISS LILLIAN. And go where?

MARY. Oh I dunno! California? Anywhere!

MISS LILLIAN. You're funny.

MARY. I'm serious! I wanna see the ocean. Big, wide, blue/

MISS LILLIAN. I'm needed here.

MARY. Oh don't it drive ya crazy?

MISS LILLIAN. Yes. No. I dunno.

MARY. You don't know?

MISS LILLIAN. Keeps me busy.

(**MARY** *nods in understanding.*)

How you doing? Sleeping yet?

MARY. Barely. A bit better. I'm fine. I'd be lost without Kid.

MISS LILLIAN. He's a tonic, it's true.

(**MISS LILLIAN** *smiles sadly.*)

MARY. You'll have your own someday.

MISS LILLIAN. .

MARY. Find you a new husband first!

MISS LILLIAN. *Mary!* I know you've never much cared for Frank, but he *is* my *husband*! And while he's still alive out there, somewhere, I/

MARY. you truly think that? About all of 'em?

MISS LILLIAN. I pray so.

(**MARY** *rolls her eyes.*)

MARY. How's that going?

MISS LILLIAN. Stop it.

MARY. I'm sure it's helping a great deal!

MISS LILLIAN. How are we friends?

MARY. God knows!

(*They kiss goodbye and* **MARY** *exits.* **MISS LILLIAN** *stands alone, still for a moment.*)

Scene Two

(Suddenly all the women are back.)

SALLY ANN. I saw it with my own eyes! As clear as the light of day. On the bible itself do I solemnly swear. By the heavens above, by the power blessed unto/

MISS LILLIAN. yes, thank you Sally Ann! Kindly tell us *what* you saw.

SALLY ANN. This morning. On the river banks, up past The Old Oaks. I saw Him!

JAYNE. You *sure* it's him?

SALLY ANN. Sure as anything ever!

LUCY. But how'd you know *exactly*?

SALLY ANN. By descriptions I've read in the newspapers.

MARY. Oh! So based in fact!

SALLY ANN. And by his image printed on that there wanted poster. *That* is the man I saw!

JAYNE. You're sure?

SALLY ANN. It was him! Stood there in front of me! Bathing and singing/

MISS LILLIAN, MARY, LUCY & JAYNE. singing?!

SALLY ANN. The most beautiful baritone. Its vibrations moved straight through my chest and near did take my breath away. I must admit that for a moment I almost forgot the man's a manifestation of the devil himself.

JAYNE. Singing and bathing?

SALLY ANN. Bathing and singing.

*(**MARY** holds up a reward poster.)*

MARY. *This* man, Sally Ann? You're sure?

SALLY ANN. Sure as sure can be. That's a very true likeness. Captures him exactly right.

LUCY. He's tall this man?

SALLY ANN. Tall, dark and handsome, it's true. Stripped to the waist and bathing in the stream. His gun belt glinting in the sunlight/

LUCY. black leather with gold buckles?

SALLY ANN. The very same. The villain must be nursing a wound, for he's bandaged all round his shoulder.

LUCY. A strong man?

SALLY ANN. Broad back and arms like tree trunks. Huge hands could lift you easy, crush you with one squeeze.

JAYNE. Oh my!

MARY. That must have been quite a sight.

SALLY ANN. It was!

MARY. Caused quite a stir.

SALLY ANN. Indeed. I saw him and with rather crushing vividness remembered the warning printed there.

LUCY. *(Reading.)* No virtuous woman is safe near Jack Cannon.

JAYNE. Oh my!

SALLY ANN. Indeed!

JAYNE. How frightening!

SALLY ANN. Yes!

JAYNE. How could you bear it Sally Ann?

SALLY ANN. I could not, truth be told. But I made an act of contrition and concentrated my thoughts upon the presence of god.

MARY. *(Sarcastic.)* Amen.

SALLY ANN. I'm praying for you Mary/

MARY. oh gawd/

MISS LILLIAN. ladies/

SALLY ANN. praying the Good Lord will change your heart/

MARY. don't bother/

MISS LILLIAN. ladies/

SALLY ANN. and praying I'll be a good example/

MARY. well you ain't!

MISS LILLIAN. Ladies please!

JAYNE. Sally Ann, when was this?

SALLY ANN. This morning. Right after I left here/

MARY. and you're only just telling us now?

SALLY ANN. I came as soon as I could! It took me nearly half the morning to recover from the shock!

JAYNE. Oh my!

SALLY ANN. That river bank had always been such a tranquil place!

JAYNE. Why, yes!

SALLY ANN. It felt as though I'd seen the devil himself!

LUCY. Well rumour is, he's magic.

MISS LILLIAN. Magic how?

LUCY. They say his music's like a spell.

SALLY ANN. Oh my!

LUCY. They say he wasn't born a man.

SALLY ANN. Oh my!

JAYNE. How queer!

MISS LILLIAN. Who is this Jack, Cannon?

JAYNE. Why! Miss Lillian?! *Everyone* knows the tale!

MISS LILLIAN. Everyone but me it'd seem.

LUCY. But *everyone* knows his name at least!

SALLY ANN. He's wanted in *fourteen* counties of this state!

JAYNE. Accused of a mighty long list of hideous crimes/

LUCY. murder! Armed robbery of citizens, state banks and post offices/

JAYNE. theft of sacred objects/

MARY. arson in a state prison/

SALLY ANN. perjury/

JAYNE. bigomy/

SALLY ANN. common indecency/

MARY. inciting prostitution/

JAYNE. kidnapping/

LUCY. extortion/

JAYNE. receiving stolen goods/

LUCY. selling stolen goods/

MARY. passing counterfeit money and/

MISS LILLIAN. OK OK! I think I get the outline of the fellow. And all this he's done alone?

LUCY. With his brother/

JAYNE & LUCY. Harry/

LUCY. until recently deceased.

MARY. The Cannon Brothers were quite the pair.

JAYNE. Tell the tale Mary!

SALLY ANN. Yes do, you tell it so good.

MARY. Harry and Jack. The Cannon Brothers, named on account of their choice of weapon. Have long been feared as the slickest gunslingers in The West/

SALLY ANN. so they say.

MARY. So they say. The aforementioned long list of crimes indicates what kind of men we're discussing here. Suggests something of their character/

SALLY ANN. villains! Manifestations of the devil himself!

MARY. Am I telling this or are you Sally Ann?

SALLY ANN. Proceed, kindly.

MARY. They robbed a stagecoach. Nothing unusual there except this was the Governor of the State, travelling with a convoy of *three* stage coaches. A small army of men protecting the Governor, important private documentation, and a pretty sum of gold coins.

MISS LILLIAN. How much?

MARY. Two hundred thousand dollars.

*(**JAYNE** whistles.)*

MISS LILLIAN. That *is* a pretty sum!

MARY. Sure is. Was a pretty robbery too, nice and neat, slick as a rat. Until it all slipped sideways.

LUCY. Sideways how?

MARY. Jack's brother Harry had hired this gang, vicious men/

SALLY ANN. God save their souls/

MARY. that go by the name of the Toothless Tommy Boys, on account of their dentistry.

LUCY. They're dentists too?

JAYNE. No dummy, they're just rotten.

LUCY. Well I don't know!

JAYNE. Clearly!

MISS LILLIAN. Girls! Carry on Mary.

MARY. Jack's brother Harry hired these Toothless Tommy Boys, to help hold up the coaches. Rumour was Harry and Jack planned to escape with the loot without paying Tommy, but now we'll never know.

MISS LILLIAN. What happened?

MARY. Well, all went well to begin with. True to his word Tommy and his toothless boys put on a show. Stopped the coach convoy in the dip of a canyon. Jack loaded his horse with the money whilst Harry and Tommy's boys held up the men. All went just as planned, 'til right at the last minute Tommy pulled his gun on Harry. Shot him straight in the face.

SALLY ANN. No!

JAYNE. No loyalty!

MARY. None at all. Tommy's boys all turned on Jack but no one's faster or more true with his aim. Jack's the slickest gunslinger in the West.

MISS LILLIAN. So they say?

MARY. So they say. Seven men shot in the time it takes to spit. And all dead before their bodies hit the ground.

JAYNE. And Tommy?

MARY. Escaped with a scratch, and a handful of men.

JAYNE. And Jack?

MARY. Disappeared in the dust.

SALLY ANN. And the money?

MARY. Who knows. Rumour is Jack buried it by moonlight way up there in the mountains. But the mountains and the moon themselves stay silent on the matter. Saddest part is Jack never got the chance to bury his brother.

LUCY. Nor Tommy bury the fallen Toothless Boys?

JAYNE. Nor the Stagecoach wives bury their men?

MARY. Their bodies left to fester in the hot sun.

SALLY ANN. And the money?

MARY. Not spent, it's getting rusty. While the desire for revenge is/

MISS LILLIAN. burning hot.

MARY. Indeed.

MISS LILLIAN. Well now, lemme get this straight. Jack's chasing the Toothless Tommy boys for revenge of his dead brother? Meanwhile *they're* chasing Jack for/

SALLY ANN. the money?

MARY. The law's chasing *all* of them for the crimes they committed/

LUCY. whilst bounty hunters are after Jack for the reward money/

JAYNE. and the press is chasing him too for the story.

MISS LILLIAN. Well! Seems the whole world's after this Jack Cannon!

MARY. They are! It's a miracle he's still breathing! Let alone bathing/

SALLY ANN. and singing!

MARY. Dead or alive, he's gotta a pretty price on his head.

MISS LILLIAN. How much?

MARY. Poster says two thousand.

LUCY. Last I heard it was three.

JACK. It's four.

(They gasp. **MISS LILLIAN** *grabs the* **SHERIFF***'s gun from the bar, but she's too slow.* **JACK** *points their gun at* **MISS LILLIAN**. *Everyone freezes.)*

I don't like shooting women.

MISS LILLIAN. Then don't.

JACK. Lower it.

MISS LILLIAN. You lower yours!

*(***JACK** *shoots a glass off a table across the room. The women duck, screaming.)*

MARY. Jesus Lillian! Drop it!

*(***MISS LILLIAN** *stares at* **JACK** *then lowers her gun to the floor.* **JACK** *motions and she kicks it over.)*

JACK. We seem to have here got off on the wrong foot. I'd like to amend that if I may?

MISS LILLIAN. .

JACK. I been on the road for some time, and I'm weary. Need a quiet place to lay my head/

SALLY ANN. not here!

JACK. I said a *quiet* place to lay my head. And this here is where I've chosen. Now if you/

MISS LILLIAN. the Sheriff's office is just right across the way! He'd have heard the shot! He'll be/

JACK. asleep, by now. In the cell I locked him in. With his favourite bottle of bourbon.

MISS LILLIAN. Dammit Roger!

JACK. Where's all the men at?

MISS LILLIAN. .

JACK. Where?

JAYNE. Out of town/

MARY. Jayne!

JACK. .

MISS LILLIAN. Out of town. On mining business.

JACK. All of 'em?!

JAYNE. All but the Sheriff.

EVERYONE EXCEPT LILLIAN. SHHH!

(Someone nudges **JAYNE** *to be quiet.)*

MISS LILLIAN. They're due back anytime now, so you'd better/

JACK. how long they been gone?

MISS LILLIAN. .

JACK. That long huh? When'd you last get word?

MISS LILLIAN. .

JACK. I see. And how you been coping with no men around/

MISS LILLIAN. just fine.

JACK. *(Smiles.)* I don't doubt it.

*(***MISS LILLIAN** *and* **JACK** *stare at each other.* **KID** *comes running in with a wooden gun.* **JACK** *almost shoots him.)*

MISS LILLIAN. Don't shoot!

MARY. He's just a boy! My boy!

KID. Stick 'em up!

JACK. You got a lot of guts kid.

KID. I sure do! You a baddie or a goodie?

JACK. Let's see. Wanna help me unsaddle my horse?

KID. Yeah!

JACK. Ask your mama.

KID. Can I? Can I mama?

*(**MARY** stares at **JACK**, surprised, then nods. **KID** celebrates and runs over to **JACK**. **JACK** lowers their gun and spins it away. **KID** stares open mouthed.)*

MISS LILLIAN. Hurt that boy and I'll kill you.

JACK. No intention of hurtin' anyone.

MISS LILLIAN. You swear?

*(**JACK** smiles, amused.)*

JACK. On the bible.

*(**MISS LILLIAN** is not amused.)*

I'm just here to rest, then I'll be on my way. How much for the room?

MISS LILLIAN. Three dollars a night. Bed and board.

JACK. A fair price. Here's a week in advance.

*(**JACK** and **KID** head for the door. **JACK** tips their hat at the ladies. **KID** copies. They exit, but **JACK** lingers on the side of the stage, his back to the women. The women explode into hushed panic.)*

SALLY ANN. Oh my god oh my god oh my/

LUCY. that was Jack Cannon/

MARY. Jesus Lillian/

LUCY. *the* Jack Cannon/

JAYNE. what are we gonna do?!

SALLY ANN. Oh my god/

MISS LILLIAN. quiet/

SALLY ANN. oh my god/

MISS LILLIAN. quiet/

SALLY ANN. oh my god/

MARY & MISS LILLIAN. *Quiet!*

MISS LILLIAN. I'm thinking! I can't think straight when you/

JAYNE. well what are we gonna do?!

MISS LILLIAN. I don't know!

SALLY ANN. He'll kill us in our sleep!

JAYNE. Unless we kill *him* in *his* sleep?!

MARY. Men like that *don't* sleep!

LUCY. He'll be too quick for us!

SALLY ANN. Oh my god oh my god/

LUCY. he's the slickest gunslinger in the West!

MARY. So they say/

MISS LILLIAN. quiet! Jesus! Will you all just quiet down for a darn minute! We need to be smart here!

(She notices her gun on the floor and picks it up.)

Mary, how many guns you got?

MARY. Two. Three including the old shotgun but I ain't never fired it.

JAYNE. Ain't none of us ever fired a gun Lillian!

LUCY. I have.

MARY. And me.

JAYNE. Well that's two of us.

SALLY ANN. Two against one!

LUCY. Not *this* one! I keep telling you he ain't like *one* man!

SALLY ANN. Oh god!

LUCY. He's like twenty!

SALLY ANN. Oh *god!*

MARY. What if he's speaking truth? When he says he's weary and/

SALLY ANN. we can't possibly *trust* him!

JAYNE. No!

MARY. Well we can't do much else?! The nearest town's over a hundred miles away!

MISS LILLIAN. We could send a telegram?

LUCY. The line's still dead from the storm. Sheriff said he'd fix it but/

MISS LILLIAN. dammit Roger!

JAYNE. We could send a letter?

LUCY. That'll take days!

SALLY ANN. We'll all be dead and buried by then!

JAYNE. Well what do you suppose we/

*(**JACK** enters the saloon followed by **KID**, bouncing with excitement.)*

KID. Did you really? Honest?!

*(**JACK** feels the vibe in the room, looks at **MISS LILLIAN** holding the gun.)*

JACK. Yeah Kid, honest. You go to your mama now. I'm hoping the lady here will show me to my room.

(**KID** *reluctantly goes to* **MARY**, *who stares at* **MISS LILLIAN.**)

MISS LILLIAN. Yes. Well. Thank you ladies, I, I don't think there's much more we can do here this evening.

SALLY ANN. Oh my god!

LUCY. If you're sure?

MISS LILLIAN. Yes, I'm sure.

SALLY ANN. Oh my god/

MISS LILLIAN. I'll see you back here in the morning, for our breakfast meeting?

JAYNE. What breakfast/

MARY. yes! The breakfast meeting!

LUCY. Yes!

SALLY ANN. Oh god/

JAYNE. yes! Breakfast/

SALLY ANN. oh my god/

(**JACK** *suddenly stretches like a cat, taking in the whole theatre, sneaking through the fourth wall. Everyone stares at* **JACK.**)

MISS LILLIAN. Right. Erm. I/

MARY. good ni/

MISS LILLIAN. good night! Yes! Good night!

LUCY. G'night.

JAYNE. G'night.

SALLY ANN. Oh! God bless us all!

(**SALLY ANN** *exits in tears followed by* **JAYNE. LUCY** *nods at* **MISS LILLIAN,** *as does* **MARY,** *an unspoken agreement. They exit.* **MISS LILLIAN,** *still holding the gun, jitters nervously.)*

MISS LILLIAN. Well then. The erm /.. The back bedroom's the largest, I suppose you, you /.. Up the stairs and on the left. And er, I'll leave fresh sheets and towels on the, on the, chair by the door in the morning and erm/

JACK. Ma'am?

MISS LILLIAN. .

JACK. Ain't no need for you to be carrying that round with you.

MISS LILLIAN. *(Quietly.)* There ain't?

(**JACK** *shakes their head.)*

Well. If it's all the same to you. I'd rather keep hold of it here.

JACK. .

MISS LILLIAN. .

JACK. Up the stairs, on the left?

MISS LILLIAN. That's it.

JACK. .

MISS LILLIAN. .

JACK. G'night ma'am.

MISS LILLIAN. G'night.

(**JACK** *stretches again.* **MISS LILLIAN** *looks away.* **JACK** *smiles, winks at us, and crosses the room.* **MISS LILLIAN** *can't watch, but feels* **JACK** *leave.* **JACK** *lingers on the edge of the stage, watching her. When she thinks* *she's alone* **MISS LILLIAN** *inhales deeply. She checks the gun, hands shaking. She paces with it. Unsure of what to do. She tries praying, gives up, and downs some bourbon. She paces again, then rushes out the door.)*

*(***JACK*** stands, walks centre stage, and takes in the whole space.* **JACK** *whistles a tune, lights a cigarette, blows smoke high into the air. They signal to a musician, inviting them to play.* **JACK** *enjoys moving their body, playing with poses and stances, an absolute rock star. They signal and the lights change, dawn rising.)*

Scene Three

(**JACK** *spins, and points their gun at the door just as the* **SHERIFF** *staggers in, hungover.)*

SHERIFF. You! You lower that weapon immediately, you hear me?! In fact get me my shotgun and I'll blow your goddamn head off with it!

JACK. Want some coffee?

SHERIFF. What?! It's my goddamn coffee! You can't offer me what's mine!

(**JACK** *walks to the bar, his gun still on the* **SHERIFF. JACK** *makes himself a tea, and pours a mug of coffee for the* **SHERIFF** *who grumbles to himself.)*

JACK. You know who I am?

SHERIFF. Sure do. And I'm gonna claim that reward money then hang you myself!

JACK. Cream or sugar?

SHERIFF. What? Both.

(**JACK** *hands the* **SHERIFF** *his coffee.)*

How do I know you ain't put poison in this?

(**JACK** *smiles and sits down.)*

That's my chair!

JACK. I'm only borrowing it. You can have it back.

(**JACK** *sips their tea. The* **SHERIFF** *stares at* **JACK**, *then sips his coffee.* **JACK** *watches. The* **SHERIFF***'s got DTs and trying to hide it.)*

SHERIFF. You won't get away with this! Can't outrun everyone forever!

JACK. .

SHERIFF. Whole world and his wife's after you!

(**JACK** *looks at the reward poster behind the bar.*)

JACK. Think that looks like me?

SHERIFF. Well it *is* you ain't it?!

JACK. I dunno. This fella's kinda got funny eyes ain't he? Think he's handsome?

(*The* **SHERIFF** *stares.* **JACK** *winks and sips their tea.*)

SHERIFF. You can't fool me. I know who you are. I know *what* you are/

JACK. that right?

SHERIFF. That's right! And I know the law!

JACK. Should hope so.

SHERIFF. You can't dress like that!

JACK. Like what?

SHERIFF. Don't play with me son! You know full well what! The law says you gotta be wearing at least two items of female clothing.

JACK. Who says I ain't? You wanna check my garters?

SHERIFF. This some game to you?!

JACK. Why, am I winning?

(**JACK** *smiles. The* **SHERIFF** *doesn't.*)

JACK. Well now look, you seem like the kind of man who knows his own mind.

SHERIFF. I do!

JACK. Who behaves how *he* sees right.

SHERIFF. That's true!

JACK. So a man like you, guided by *his* truth, wouldn't be threatened by something as flimsy as fabric.

SHERIFF. What's your point son?

JACK. Material's just material. Man adds the meaning. And man should be free to dress his own body as he chooses. To truly ask himself his preference, and then honour that. So, Sheriff, don't your skin fancy a bit of silk sometimes?

SHERIFF. Get outta here! Go on, get!

*(**JACK** chuckles into their tea. The **SHERIFF** mumbles to himself.)*

JACK. I've never seen a town like this. Black people, white people, all living together? Getting on fine?

SHERIFF. Frank's rules.

JACK. Frank?

SHERIFF. The man who built this saloon you're sleeping in. Good Miss Lillian's husband. He's got two rules. No guns, no politics.

JACK. Good rules. Except there's always both.

SHERIFF. Not here! This is a good town! We built it so, and we work hard to keep it so!

*(The **SHERIFF** suddenly falls quiet. **JACK** watches.)*

JACK. How many went?

SHERIFF. Ninety-two men. The gals are still hopeful of their return.

JACK. And you?

SHERIFF. Can't say.

*(**JACK** sits quietly, thinking. The **SHERIFF** tries to sip his coffee with shaky hands, spills it down himself. Looks up to catch **JACK** watching.)*

Gonna laugh at me?

JACK. No sir.

SHERIFF. .

*(**JACK** looks behind the bar.)*

JACK. We had a horse. When I was little. Was a fine beast, 'til he started shaking one day. And once he started he couldn't stop/

SHERIFF. they put him down?

*(**JACK** finds a half quart of whiskey. **JACK** pours a big glug in the **SHERIFF**'s mug without looking at him. **JACK** replaces the bottle and sits back down.)*

JACK. I won't be here long. I come to rest, then I'll be on my way. Now look, I know it's your duty to report me, and I don't wanna interrupt your duty sir, I really don't/

SHERIFF. then don't.

JACK. I'm just hoping you might, delay it, a while.

SHERIFF. Oh! So you can spend your stolen gold?!

JACK. No/

SHERIFF. on liquor and women, no doubt?

JACK. No/

SHERIFF. a fast horse, and fancy men's clothes/

JACK. no! I don't care about the money!

SHERIFF. Sure! Don't care 'bout your famous name either?! Want me to ignore my duty as a man of the law so you can swan around and/

JACK. that's not what I'm asking, honest! Look, I got a *job* to do!

SHERIFF. Woah now, I can't be hearing this/

JACK. and it's likely gonna get me killed/

SHERIFF. then you better reconsider/

JACK. but I gotta do it regardless/

SHERIFF. you don't gotta do nothing/

JACK. they shot my brother! They /..

(A wave of grief suddenly crashes over **JACK.** *The* **SHERIFF** *is softer, tender even. Then suddenly* **JACK***'s wall is back up.)*

But first I gotta rest. I got a bullet hole here to fix up, and with everyone's chasing me up and down the desert, raising the ransom sky high and printing posters that look *nothin' like me*, I can't get much restin' done! Just a little pause, that's all I'm asking.

SHERIFF. And in return?

JACK. I'll tell you two things.

SHERIFF. Where the money's hid?

*(***JACK** *nods and stands.)*

And?

JACK. How we healed that shaking horse.

*(***JACK** *walks to the door.)*

*(***JAYNE** *suddenly appears.)*

JAYNE. Oh! Good afternoon Mr. Cannon. Sheriff.

*(**JACK** looks at the **SHERIFF** who nods. The **SHERIFF** tips his hat at **JAYNE** who smiles politely. The **SHERIFF** exits. **JAYNE** gets flustered.)*

JACK. Ma'am?

JAYNE. Well now, Mr. Cannon, I was wondering if you might be so kind as to assist me? It's just the schoolyard fence is bust right through and, well I just can't seem to manage all by myself. I know it's bold of me to ask but, well, seens as you're here?

JACK. I'd be happy to.

JAYNE. You will? Oh my! I just knew you would!

SALLY ANN. Jayne?!

*(**SALLY ANN** and **LUCY** have suddenly appeared. They're staring open mouthed at **JAYNE** and **JACK**.)*

JAYNE. Good afternoon Sally Ann, Miss Lucy.

LUCY. Good after/

SALLY ANN. *what* are you doing?!

JAYNE. Nothing! I /..

JACK. .

JAYNE. Mr. Cannon here has kindly agreed to help mend the schoolyard fence!

SALLY ANN. .

JAYNE. Isn't that kind?

SALLY ANN. .

LUCY. I can mend it myself.

JAYNE. *(Laughs high pitched.)* Oh no don't be silly, Miss Lucy! We can't have *you*, mending *fences!*

LUCY. Why not?

(**JAYNE** *laughs, too loudly.*)

I'm perfectly capable/

JAYNE. well you ain't! I asked Mr. Cannon here and he said yes, so that's that!

JACK. I've no tools.

JAYNE. I can get you some! Or you can borrow whatever you'd need from Lucy's farm. Isn't that right, Miss Lucy?

LUCY. Sure.

(**SALLY ANN** *stares at them all, stunned.*)

JACK. I'll write you a list. Drop it round tomorrow morning?

JAYNE. Wonderful! Ooh, I'll make us breakfast!

SALLY ANN. *(Explodes.) Breakfast?!*

JACK. Just coffee, ma'am, thank you.

(**JACK** *tips their hat.* **JAYNE** *and* **LUCY** *curtsy.* **SALLY ANN** *scowls.* **JACK** *suddenly does a cheeky little dance move for* **SALLY ANN**, *who's horrified.* **JAYNE** *and* **LUCY** *are delighted.*)

Ladies.

(**JACK** *exits, lingering in the shadows watching the scene*)

SALLY ANN. Jayne Goodfellow?! What on *earth* are you doing?

JAYNE. What on earth are *you* doing being so rude?!

SALLY ANN. Have you forgotten who that is?!

JAYNE. He's mighty handsome ain't he?

SALLY ANN. He's an *outlaw!* A *bandit!* He's not to be *complimented!* Or *trusted* or any other thing!

JAYNE. What other thing could you be considering there Sally Ann?

*(**LUCY** snorts a laugh.)*

Cus I can think of plenty.

LUCY & SALLY ANN. *Jayne!*

JAYNE. What?

SALLY ANN. You're *engaged!* To be *married!*

JAYNE. And you're a boring old trout!

SALLY ANN. Goodness!

JAYNE. Oh it's been so long since I've seen a man, you can't blame a girl for looking a little! Ain't that right Lucy?

LUCY. I guess.

SALLY ANN. Goodness!

JAYNE. Oh good day Sally Ann! Come on Lucy!

LUCY. Good day!

*(**SALLY ANN** is left alone and starts uttering prayers.)*

Scene Four

*(***JACK*** stands and turns to face* **SALLY ANN**. **JACK** *tips their hat to her. She stares at him, terrified, and backs away carefully, then sprints off.* **JACK** *shrugs to us, stretches a little, looks around.* **JACK** *spots the piano in the corner of the saloon. He can't resist it.* **JACK** *begins to play something, then suddenly spins and is pointing his gun across the saloon. Silence and stillness, before two little hands appear behind the bar.* **JACK** *exhales and spins his gun away.* **KID** *pokes his head out.)*

KID. Don't shoot!

JACK. You ain't meant to be in here.

KID. You ain't meant to have no guns in here!

*(***JACK*** sits back at the piano.* **KID** *walks over to him.)*

I know you still got one. I know you got *two!*

*(***JACK*** winks at* **KID**. **KID** *stares.* **JACK** *starts to play something.)*

I know who you are!

JACK. That right?

KID. They say you're an outlaw! They say you're chasing to kill a man before he kills you! They say/

JACK. they say a lot! Don't they? Even when they know so little.

KID. They say/

JACK. shush little one. I've got a song brewin' and you're 'bout to steal the lick right outta my/

KID. this ain't the time for writing songs! You gotta go get revenge!

JACK. That so?

KID. Yes! For your dead brother!

JACK. Well now, you seem to know plenty 'bout it.

KID. I do. And I know what you gotta do. You gotta kill Tommy, and *all* his Toothless Boys, before they kill you. *And* you gotta kill *all* the bounty hunters that are chasing you for the reward money! *And* you've gotta do *all* that but not get caught by the law!

JACK. That all sounds mighty complicated.

KID. Yeah but, you're *thee* Jack Cannon! You're gonna win!

JACK. Reckon so?

KID. *Yes!*

JACK. How'd you know for sure?

KID. Ah that's easy! Cus you're a good-bad-guy!

JACK. What's a good-bad-guy?

KID. A bad guy who's actually good. Or a good guy who does bad things, but only cus he *has* to. Or a bad guy who *does* bad things but *underneath* is really a good guy.

JACK. *(Genuine.)* And I'm one of them?

KID. Yeah! But don't worry, I won't tell no one. They'll work it out, *eventually!*

JACK. How did you know?

KID. Oh.

*(**KID** looks at us, taking us all in. **JACK** smiles, unsurprised **KID** can see us.)*

It's obvious!

JACK. Is it?

KID. Yeah! It's all over your face when you smile! In your eyes. Look!

*(**KID** holds **JACK**'s face really close to his own. They stare into each others eyes.)*

(Whispers.) See?

JACK. *(Whispers.)* Yeah!

MARY. *(Calls off stage.)* Kid?! Kid?!

*(**KID** moves away from **JACK. JACK** winks at **KID. KID** tries to wink back but can't manage it. **MARY** enters.)*

There you are! Oh, Mr. Cannon! I hope he wasn't/

JACK. he's fine.

MARY. Where's everyone at?

*(**JACK** shrugs. **MISS LILLIAN** enters and stares at **JACK. JACK** moves away from the piano, suddenly embarrassed.)*

MISS LILLIAN. Oh! Do you *play* Mr. Cannon?! Then you must play for us! Ain't that right, Mary?

MARY. Wh-why yes!

JACK. Maybe.

*(**JAYNE, SALLY ANN** and **LUCY** enter.)*

JAYNE. Oh, Mr. Cannon!

SALLY ANN. *(Hissed.)* Jayne!

JACK. Ladies.

*(**JACK** tips their hat. The women curtsy. **JACK** moves downstage to start sawing some

wood. As soon as **JACK***'s gone they burst into fevered whispers.)*

MISS LILLIAN. *(Loud whisper.)* Oh my! I don't think my heart can take it!

MARY. *(Loud whisper.)* You're doing fine!

SALLY ANN. *(Loud whisper.)* What is he doing?!

JAYNE. *(Loud whisper.)* Fixing the fence.

MARY. Well, thank god for Mr. Cannon.

MISS LILLIAN & SALLY ANN. *(Hissed.)* Thank god?!

MARY. Well, that fence has needed fixing for/

MISS LILLIAN. yes but can we *trust* him?!

MARY. Careful now, you're sounding just like Miss Sally Ann.

SALLY ANN. I'm merely interested in the protection of this town and its, its...

(They all get distracted by something **JACK** *is doing.)*

MARY. Well, you sure do seem mighty interested in the fellow.

JAYNE, SALLY ANN & MISS LILLIAN. No I don't!

MISS LILLIAN. Oh what are we going to do?!

SALLY ANN. I don't know!

MISS LILLIAN. Well *think!* We need an escape plan! And *fast!*

LUCY. I don't know, he seems kind of fine to me?

SALLY ANN & MISS LILLIAN. Kind of fine?!

SALLY ANN. He's a *bandit!*

JAYNE. He's handsome as hell!

MARY. As hell is right. Don't forget who the man is/

MISS LILLIAN. exactly!

LUCY. I'm just saying he *seems* fine/

JAYNE. and handsome!

MISS LILLIAN. Oh *shut up* about how *handsome* he is!

JAYNE. Oh so you agree then?

MISS LILLIAN. Yes! No! It, it doesn't matter/

SALLY ANN. the point is he could murder us in our beds/

MISS LILLIAN. yes/

MARY. he *is* an outlaw/

MISS LILLIAN. yes/

SALLY ANN. and *not* to be trusted! Oh he makes me so uneasy!

JAYNE. Oh, and me!

LUCY. Jayne!

JAYNE. What?!

MISS LILLIAN. It seems like everyone's clear forgot exactly who the man is! ... I mean, is *man* the right /.. I don't mean to, I just, none of the words quite /.. I've never met anyone like Jack.

MARY. Lillian, are you blushing?

MISS LILLIAN. No!

JAYNE & MARY. You are!

MISS LILLIAN. *No!*

SALLY ANN, LUCY, JAYNE & MARY. You *are!*

MISS LILLIAN. *You* are!

(They all giggle like school girls then stop themselves, as **JACK** *crosses the saloon with the saw.)*

I want you ladies to keep your distance/

SALLY ANN. yes/

MISS LILLIAN. keep your wits about you/

SALLY ANN. yes/

MISS LILLIAN. and keep your misguided compliments to yourselves.

KID. Bang bang bang!

MISS LILLIAN. And keep that boy away from him!

MARY. Don't you tell me how to raise my son!

MISS LILLIAN. I wasn't! I was just/

MARY. come here Kid we're goin'!

MISS LILLIAN. Oh Mary, don't!

*(***MARY** *grabs* **KID** *and drags him out of the saloon.* **JAYNE** *pouts and preens.* **LUCY** *watches her, amused.* **MISS LILLIAN** *suddenly looks exhausted.)*

Go home, go home

LUCY. Some mighty fine saloon this is!

JAYNE. Turning away regular customers? Well!

SALLY ANN. Well indeed!

*(***SALLY ANN** *storms off.)*

*(***JAYNE** *and* **LUCY** *strut out.* **MISS LILLIAN** *almost breathes a sigh of relief when the* **SHERIFF** *bursts in.)*

SHERIFF. Ah! Miss Lillian!

MISS LILLIAN. Not tonight Sheriff I really don't have the steam for it.

SHERIFF. Now Miss Lillian/

MISS LILLIAN. is it one bottle or two?

*(***MISS LILLIAN** *pulls three bottles out of a box and puts them on the bar.)*

SHERIFF. Well now, I/

MISS LILLIAN. There, that's all we've got. Take them with you and we'll settle it tomorrow.

SHERIFF. *(Embarrassed.)* Well! This is what I call express service!

MISS LILLIAN. G'night Sheriff.

(The **SHERIFF** *doesn't take the bottles but* **LILLIAN** *doesn't notice. He leaves, tipping his hat as he goes.)*

Scene Five

*(**MISS LILLIAN** locks the door and closes the shutters. She kicks off her shoes and collapses into an armchair. She gets approximately thirty seconds of sweet peace before **JACK** is suddenly there. They stare at each other. She suddenly bursts into action, putting on her shoes whilst patting down her hair.)*

MISS LILLIAN. Forgive me, I/

JACK. no! There's no need. Stay as you are.

*(She gingerly sits back in the chair. **JACK** passes her a cup of tea. She stares, surprised. **JACK** sips theirs. She takes a sip, it tastes perfect. **JACK** smiles.)*

You seem surprised.

MISS LILLIAN. I am.

JACK. Pleasantly?

MISS LILLIAN. .

JACK. .

MISS LILLIAN. Well! Well, perhaps there is some decency in you after all/

JACK. wouldn't count on that ma'am.

MISS LILLIAN. No?

JACK. No. I'd only disappoint you.

*(**MISS LILLIAN** fizzes. **JACK** doesn't look away.)*

MISS LILLIAN. Do you, like tea, Mr. Cannon?

*(**JACK** smiles.)*

Well I suppose you do, you're drinking it ain't ya! How foolish of me!

JACK. .

MISS LILLIAN. I suppose you're quite used to/

JACK. we don't got to speak no small talk, Ma'am. Don't gotta speak nothin' at all. Can just enjoy the quiet here, together.

(They sit quietly sipping their tea. **JACK** *watches her. She blushes.* **JACK** *smiles. She blushes some more.* **JACK** *finishes their cup and places it down on the table.* **JACK** *stands.* **MISS LILLIAN** *can't watch, but feels* **JACK** *walk across the saloon to the piano. She inhales deeply, dizzy.* **JACK** *starts playing, tinkering on the piano. The band joins in and takes over. The sound makes* **MISS LILLIAN** *stand. She walks to the mirror behind the bar. She takes down her hair, and puts it half-up in a red ribbon. She smiles to herself, and enjoys moving her body in a gentle sway.* **JACK** *dances, wild and free. The stage fills with people. The sound infects everyone. They move their bodies, exploring the shapes they can make. Their skin seems to be defrosting, revealing dormant desire. It's delicious, and a bit scary.* **JACK** *stops dancing and everyone freezes. They brush it away like nothing happened. The* **SHERIFF**, **KID**, **LUCY** *and* **SALLY ANN** *exit.)*

Scene Six

MARY. Well, good morning Miss Lillian!

MISS LILLIAN. Good morning Mary, Jayne, Sally Ann, Lucy. What can I do for you/

JAYNE. why Miss Lillian! Your hair!

MISS LILLIAN. What about it?

JAYNE. Well it looks awful pretty!

MISS LILLIAN. Why, thank you.

MARY. So it does. What's the occasion?

MISS LILLIAN. No occasion. I just, thought I'd try somethin' new.

*(**JACK** stands. **MISS LILLIAN** tries not to blush.)*

Oh! Mr. Cannon! Good morning.

JAYNE & MARY. Good morning.

JACK. Ladies.

JAYNE. Don't she look awful pretty Mr. Cannon?

JACK. Who?

JAYNE. Why Miss Lillian! With her new hairdo.

MISS LILLIAN. *(Hissed.)* Jayne.

JACK. I hadn't noticed.

JAYNE. Well look now! Ain't it pretty?

JACK. Very.

*(**MISS LILLIAN** blushes. **JACK** smiles. **JAYNE** smirks, watching them. **MARY**'s jaw hits the floor.)*

MISS LILLIAN. Well now! We should let Mr. Cannon be on his way. I'm sure he's very busy/

JAYNE. very!

JACK. .

MISS LILLIAN. .

JACK. .

JAYNE. .

MARY. .

MISS LILLIAN. Was there anything else Jayne? Mary? Sally Ann? Lucy? No? Good. Please collect whatever flour or sugar or salt it is you've come to borrow a cup of and kindly be on your way.

MARY. Well I'll be!

MISS LILLIAN. You know where it is. And kindly please don't take more than you need. I've got a watchful eye on the inventory of those shelves and monitor exactly what's coming and going.

JAYNE. That ain't the only thing she's got a watchful eye on.

(They exit giggling, leaving **JACK** *to smile at us.)*

Scene Seven

*(**JACK**, half-dressed, is wetting down their hair in the mirror. **LUCY** enters.)*

LUCY. Oh I'm sorry!

JACK. Don't be.

*(**JACK** motions for **LUCY** to enter. She does, shyly. **JACK** pulls on a shirt and does up the buttons, **LUCY** watches.)*

LUCY. Uh, Miss Jayne is wondering if you'd be joining us this evening? It's just she'd like to buy you a drink, to thank you for mending the fence.

JACK. Tell her it ain't necessary. But yeah, I'll be there, for a bit.

LUCY. Good, that's good.

*(**LUCY** hovers by the door watching **JACK**. **JACK** considers the gaze, feeling it out. **LUCY** blushes.)*

Forgive me! It's just. Have you always dressed this way?

JACK. Since I was a young 'un.

LUCY. .

JACK. All these, petticoats, and the like? Never did make much sense on my body.

*(**JACK** now dressed, looks at themselves in the mirror, is content. Enjoys a dance move, comfortable expressing themself. **LUCY** stares.)*

LUCY. And the confidence? To just walk out this way?

JACK. Is it confidence if it's necessary?

*(**LUCY** stares. **JACK** throws her his hat. She shyly puts it on, closes her eyes, smiles. **KID** runs in and she hides it behind her back.)*

KID. Jack! Jack! You coming?

JACK. Sure.

KID. *Yesssss!*

JACK. You go on now, I'll follow you.

*(**JACK** takes the hat from **LUCY** and pats her on the shoulder as they leave. **LUCY** looks around the room, feels one of **JACK**'s shirts, looks at herself in the mirror. She turns away frowning.)*

Scene Eight

(The bar is suddenly busy. Everyone is sat around drinking quietly, and playing cards. Someone is tinkling on the piano. **MARY** *gets an idea.)*

MARY. Hey! Howdie there partner! You know it's customary in this here town that people travelling through treat us to a tune.

JACK. That right?

MARY. The band's pretty versatile.

JACK. I'm sorry to disappoint you, ma'am/

MARY. you won't disappoint me nothin' if you get up there and show us what you got.

MISS LILLIAN. *(Hissed.)* Mary!

MARY. Come on little songbird, everyone's got a tune in 'em.

JACK. That right?

MARY. Sure is.

JACK. Maybe later.

MARY. Sure. How 'bout now?

MISS LILLIAN. Mary!

JACK. Ma'am, I /

MARY. no? OK... How 'bout now?

MISS LILLIAN. Let him be Mary.

JAYNE. Yeah Mary. Don't embarrass the man.

MARY. Hell! You're right, I forgot some cowboys just ain't got the stomach for it.

JAYNE. That so?

MARY. Sure is. Maybe Mr. Cannon here is kinda jelly legs.

MISS LILLIAN. *Mary!*

JAYNE. Maybe he is!

MARY. And if he is, we shouldn't mock the poor fellow.

JAYNE. Oh no! It's not his fault if he's jelly legs.

MARY. No! Tragic really.

JAYNE. Tragic!

MARY. Some cowboys walk just don't match their talk.

JAYNE. Ain't that the truth!

*(**JACK** suddenly stands, and walks over to the band. They start playing. **JACK** sings something bluesy and contemporary, it's a sound that no one has heard before. **JACK**'s performance is quite clearly for **MISS LILLIAN**. She struggles not to blush, but doesn't look away. Halfway through the song **JACK** throws the mic to **MARY**, who picks up the song. **JACK** walks through the bar. Everyone they pass is somehow changed by the music, swept up in it. Their movement grows, and they lift their eyes to see each other. They witness the defrosting in each other. **JACK** sits on the bar watching them all. The song ends. They wake from the spell and find themselves in unexpected positions. They brush the event away, laugh it off, down a shot. The piano tinkles politely again like before. Everyone but **JACK** and **LUCY** exit.)*

Scene Nine

*(**LUCY** is undressed to their underwear, decidedly not looking in the mirror. **JACK** is smoking, and watching **LUCY** pull on a man's shirt, pull up some braces, shyly try on a hat. **LUCY** stands before **JACK**, feeling exposed.)*

JACK. There now! Quite the handsome chap ain't ya.

LUCY. Am I?

JACK. Take a look for yourself.

*(**JACK** gestures to the mirror but **LUCY** doesn't move towards it.)*

LUCY. *(Shyly.)* I don't seem, foolish, to you?

JACK. Foolish? Well now. Stand up straight, lemme look at you.

*(**JACK** stands in front of **LUCY**. Tidies her braces, holds her shoulders, stands back to take a look at her. She bites her lip.)*

You seem strong to me.

*(**LUCY** smiles shyly, takes a deep breath, looks in the mirror. **LUCY** looks for a long time. **JACK** watches.)*

What's it look like to you?

LUCY. Like my outsides match my insides.

*(They smile at each other in understanding. **JAYNE** suddenly bursts in followed closely by **MISS LILLIAN**. **LUCY** burns and whips off the hat.)*

MISS LILLIAN. Oh/

JAYNE. oh my!

*(**JAYNE** stares. **MISS LILLIAN** is faster to kindness.)*

MISS LILLIAN. Well now, who's this handsome one?

LOU. I'm Lou.

JACK. Lou. This, is Lou.

*(**MISS LILLIAN** extends her hand for **LOU** to kiss.)*

MISS LILLIAN. How'd you do sir?

LOU. Ma'am.

*(**LOU** kisses **MISS LILLIAN**'s hand and she curtsys. **JAYNE** stares, then suddenly curtsys at **LOU** too. **LOU** nods their head at them, smiling shyly. **JAYNE** stares at **LOU**.)*

MISS LILLIAN. I'm sorry to intrude on you gentlemen, but Miss Jayne here was quite insistent. Now, what was it, that was so urgent Miss Jayne?

JAYNE. .

MISS LILLIAN. Jayne?

JAYNE. *(Quietly, staring at **LOU**.)* Oh it hardly matters now.

MISS LILLIAN. Right! Well, in that case, perhaps we should leave these gentlemen in peace? ... Jayne?

*(**JAYNE** stares at **LOU**, blushes, and runs out the room. **JACK** looks at **MISS LILLIAN**, smiling. She smiles back.)*

My apologies again, gentleman.

JACK. Ma'am.

*(**MISS LILLIAN** exits. **LOU** and **JACK** burst into a fit of giggles.)*

LOU. Gee! I don't think my heart can take it all at once!

JACK. Well it's done now!

LOU. So it is!

*(**LOU** looks at themselves in the mirror.)*

Lou, I'm Lou, I'm Louie. Howdie, I'm Lou. Gee!

JACK. Feel good?

LOU. Good? The *best!* Feels *right* you know?

JACK. I do.

LOU. Did you see their faces?!

JACK. I saw Jayne's.

*(**LOU** blushes hard. **JACK** laughs.)*

Easy tiger. One step at a time.

*(**KID** bursts in.)*

KID. Jack! Jack! You wanna come outside and, *(Spots **LOU**.)* why you dressed like that?

*(**LOU** holds their breath.)*

JACK. Kid, this is Lou. That's how they dress now.

KID. Oh, OK. Hi Lou. You coming outside Jack?

JACK. Sure Kid, you go down and I'll follow you.

*(**KID** runs outside. **LOU** exhales. **JACK** walks through the bar, whistling. **MISS LILLIAN** enters as **LOU** exits.)*

MISS LILLIAN. The Sheriff's looking for you. And to my great surprise I do believe he's *sober?!* Said something 'bout a shaking horse?

JACK. I got it.

(**JACK** *goes to leave.)*

MISS LILLIAN. Miss Davies said thank you for the recipe. The drummer said you were right about the two and the four. Miss Baxter's hoping you'll fix her fence like you did the schoolyard. And Kid's out front waiting to play.

JACK. Right, thanks.

(**JACK** *goes to leave.)*

MISS LILLIAN. Fitting right in ain't ya? Turning this whole town upside down!

JACK. I ain't staying long. Be out your hair in no time.

(**JACK** *goes to leave but comes back.)*

That was really great just now, what you did. For Lou.

MISS LILLIAN. Oh, it was nothin'.

JACK. It was plenty.

MISS LILLIAN. You seem surprised.

JACK. I am.

MISS LILLIAN. Pleasantly?

JACK. .

MISS LILLIAN. Well, just don't go painting me up in your mind as some pretty little housewife.

JACK. No?

MISS LILLIAN. No. I'll only disappoint you.

JACK. Hope so.

(They stare at each other. **MISS LILLIAN** *fizzes.* **JACK** *smiles.* **MISS LILLIAN** *exits. The* **SHERIFF** *staggers in.)*

Scene Ten

*(**JACK** half-walks half-carries the **SHERIFF** into the saloon and plonks him down on a chair. The **SHERIFF** is detoxing. It's not pretty. **JACK** checks his pulse.)*

SHERIFF. Itchy. It's all, itchy and /..

JACK. What you got here? Coffee?

SHERIFF. Just coffee! I swear! That's all I/

JACK. OK OK, let's put a little drop of whiskey/

SHERIFF. no! No!

JACK. We gotta taper you off Sheriff. Can't just stop or you get sick. Come on now. Little sips.

*(The **SHERIFF** reluctantly drinks.)*

SHERIFF. What kind of man, gets himself /.. You think I'm weak! Stupid?!

JACK. I think you're strong.

SHERIFF. Ha! /

JACK. You're strong, *and*, you're sick. So we're gonna fix you up, you hear me? Drink this.

*(The **SHERIFF** struggles to keep it down, squirms in shame. **JACK**'s actions are simple and kind.)*

SHERIFF. Tell me 'bout the horse.

JACK. Oh he's a beauty all right. Mighty, 'n' magnificent. Real solid in the body, fast. Secret to him was how gentle he could be. You wouldn't think it to look at him but, when the timing was right? He could be real gentle. Broke my heart when he got sick. Prayed over and over he'd pull through. Prayed to a god I ain't never believed in. My daddy paid an old medicine man to fix up a tincture. Dunno if it was that or my prayers but, one morning he woke up good as new, maybe even stronger than before.

(The **SHERIFF** *falls asleep.* **JACK** *holds him and hums a song. The song infects the band, and they start playing. The sound draws* **MISS LILLIAN** *to* **JACK**. *She stands before him, trying to not look flustered. The* **SHERIFF** *stands and exits.* **JACK** *stands and stares at* **MISS LILLIAN**. *She doesn't know where to look.* **JACK** *walks slowly across the room to her. She tries to keep eye contact but can't take the pressure and at the last minute turns her body away from him.* **JACK** *stands right next to her, and waits. She tries to breathe.* **JACK** *waits, and waits. Suddenly she turns and almost kisses* **JACK**, *but the door bursts open and* **SALLY ANN** *enters. The music cuts and* **JACK** *and* **MISS LILLIAN** *spring apart.)*

Scene Eleven

SALLY ANN. Ah Miss Lillian, oh Mr. Cannon! I didn't see you there! I can come back later.

MISS LILLIAN. No Sally Ann you're welcome now, what can I do for you?

SALLY ANN. Well it's about the pastor. I was thinking it couldn't hurt for us to send a follow-up letter, it's been over three months now after all/

MISS LILLIAN. of course/

SALLY ANN. I don't think anyone could accuse us of being too hasty in our correspondence. We've been patient long enough!

MISS LILLIAN. Yes/

SALLY ANN. and the need is of course of the utmost urgency!

MISS LILLIAN. Of course/

SALLY ANN. so I feel that perhaps a follow-up letter could help to, nudge, things along.

MISS LILLIAN. Right, yes/

SALLY ANN. oh I knew you'd agree. I brought some parchment and a pencil just like before.

MISS LILLIAN. Now? You want to write it now?

SALLY ANN. Unless it's terribly inconvenient to you?

(**JAYNE** *bursts in.*)

JAYNE. Goddammit my stitching's come undone again! May I borrow your needle and thread Miss Lillian? I've been doing it how you taught me but I oh! Mr. Cannon!

JACK. Ladies.

(**JACK** *tips their hat and exits to sit on the stairs.* **JACK** *stares at* **MISS LILLIAN**, *who burns.)*

JAYNE. Where's your sewing kit at/

SALLY ANN. we could begin like the last one/

JAYNE. Miss Lillian/

SALLY ANN. if it suits you?

MISS LILLIAN. Yes, right no, sorry. I'm sorry ladies but I've got an awful headache.

JAYNE. Oh no!

MISS LILLIAN. I know/

SALLY ANN. oh you poor thing!

JAYNE. You do look a bit peaky.

MISS LILLIAN. I'm sorry but I need to close up for the evening and go lie down.

SALLY ANN. Yes of course! Put a cold compress on/

JAYNE. and cover your lamps!

SALLY ANN. Yes! Cover them to dim the room!

MISS LILLIAN. Thank you, I'll do that. I'm terribly sorry to let you both down.

JAYNE. Gee don't you worry 'bout us. We'll be fine for one evening!

SALLY ANN. Yes yes! Go! Go and rest/

JAYNE. you go lay down/

SALLY ANN. we'll be back to check on you in the morning

MISS LILLIAN. Thank you. You're very kind.

JAYNE. G'night Miss Lillian/

SALLY ANN. good night! God bless/

MISS LILLIAN. g'night!

*(***MISS LILLIAN*** locks the door behind her and runs to the stairs. She runs to the mirror and checks her appearance. She runs back to the stairs. She runs to the bar and downs a shot. Downs some more, straight out the bottle. She runs to the stairs. She slows herself down to ascend them like a lady. She looks up and* **JACK***'s on their way down. They meet mid-way up and stare at each other nose to nose.)*

JACK. Can I kiss you?

MISS LILLIAN. Yes!

*(***JACK*** kisses her. They tumble into kisses. It's urgent and hot. Eventually she breaks away.)*

Wait! Wait here.

(She rushes offstage. She pulls on a massive metal bathtub. It's heavy, the water sloshing about inside. She undresses quickly to her underwear. Halfway through she starts trying to undress sexily, then gives up and strips quickly. She gets in the tub, poses a few different ways, before deciding what feels right. **JACK** *hasn't moved, hasn't stopped smiling.)*

OK.

*(***JACK*** doesn't move, stood smiling. She waits. Then* **JACK** *walks towards her and climbs in the tub with their clothes on. She squeals and laughs.* **JACK** *lays on top of her.)*

JACK. Can I kiss you?

*(***MISS LILLIAN*** kisses* **JACK***. The lights fade over the next section of text, and a blue neon*

light inside the bathtub slowly glows brighter. Urgent kissing and touching.)

Can I /..

MISS LILLIAN. Yes!

JACK. Can I /..

MISS LILLIAN. Yes!

JACK. Can I/

MISS LILLIAN. yes!

JACK. Can I/

MISS LILLIAN. yes!

JACK. Yes!

MISS LILLIAN. Yes!

JACK. Yes!

MISS LILLIAN. Yes!

JACK. Yes!

MISS LILLIAN. Yes!

JACK. Yes!

MISS LILLIAN & JACK. Yes! Yes! Yes! Yes! Yes! Yes! Yes!

(Blackout except the neon, like they're floating in blue. The rest of the world disappears as they zone in on each other, drunk on love. Their language seems different here too, more contemporary somehow. What follows next is a kaleidoscope of snapshot scenes. Dizzy and delicious. It's a dance, but not pretty. It's erotic and passionate, but honest and messy. The blue neon bath light fades and glows, hazy and intoxicating.)

(They are all over each other, greedy for skin. **MISS LILLIAN** *jumps up so her legs are wrapped around* **JACK**'s *waist. They spin and she squeals. Blackout.)*

(Lights up. **JACK** *is stood behind* **MISS LILLIAN**, *arms wrapped around her, kissing her neck. They sway in lust. Blackout.)*

(Lights up. **JACK** *is next to the bathtub, dancing, smoking.* **MISS LILLIAN** *is laying in the tub watching.)*

MISS LILLIAN. More! More! More!

(Blackout.)

(Lights up. **MISS LILLIAN** *is stood in the tub dancing.* **JACK** *is outside the tub dancing. The same moves but physically separate, their eyes on each other. Blackout.)*

(Lights up. **MISS LILLIAN** *is stood still, one foot up on the side of the tub.* **JACK** *is knelt down on the floor, kissing her thighs.* **JACK** *takes great care to make sure they've covered every single inch in tiny kisses. She watches, breathing deeply. Blackout.)*

(Lights up. **JACK** *is laying on his back.* **MISS LILLIAN** *is dancing on the side of the bath for* **JACK**. *Her powerful feminine energy on full display.* **JACK** *reaches a hand out to touch her, she dances away from him.* **JACK** *tries again and she bats his hand away. Eventually he can't bear not touching her, and jumps to his feet to grab her. She squeals in delight and faux surprise. She pushes him down and climbs on top of him. They laugh. They kiss. A tangle of limbs and water. Blackout.)*

(Lights up. **JACK** *is laying in the bath with* **MISS LILLIAN** *lying asleep on his chest.* **JACK** *is smoking, pointing their gun at us. Blackout.)*

(Lights up. **JACK** *is asleep in* **MISS LILLIAN***'s arms. She is stroking his hair, smoking, holding the gun, staring at us. Blackout.)*

(Lights up. They're all over each other, greedy for skin. Blackout.)

(Lights up. **MISS LILLIAN** *is stood in the tub with* **JACK***'s gun and is furious.* **JACK** *runs and cowers as she points it at him.)*

Say that again!

JACK. .

MISS LILLIAN. Say it! Say it! *Say it!*

JACK. .

(Blackout.)

(Lights up. They're sat in the tub, staring at each other, their left palms touching, the water dripping down their arms. **JACK** *stares at her.)*

MISS LILLIAN. What?

JACK. Nothin'.

MISS LILLIAN. .

JACK. What?

MISS LILLIAN. Nothin'.

(They smile. **JACK** *hums part of a song, and softly sings a lyric.)*

What's that? Something new?

JACK. Maybe. Sort of drifts in and out.

*(**JACK** looks at **MISS LILLIAN**'s hands. They watch the water drip off. **JACK** licks and kisses them. She moans softly.)*

MISS LILLIAN. Can we stay here forever?

JACK. You'll get all wrinkly.

MISS LILLIAN. Don't care. You'll still love me.

JACK. .

MISS LILLIAN. Hey!

(They play fight. Laughter and water everywhere. Blackout.)

*(Lights up. They're kissing, getting out of the tub and onto a nest of towels. The intensity increases. **JACK** holds **MISS LILLIAN**'s arms up behind her head and kisses her neck.)*

(Blurts out.) I want your child!

JACK. .

MISS LILLIAN. Sorry. Sorry! I /.. That was, stupid, really fucking stupid/

JACK. no! Impossible maybe, but not /..

MISS LILLIAN. .

JACK. .

MISS LILLIAN. .

JACK. Look, if I could.

*(**JACK** gets frustrated, ashamed maybe. She tries to soothe him.)*

MISS LILLIAN. Hey. It's OK!

JACK. It's not! It's not OK/

MISS LILLIAN. no/

JACK. it's fucking cruel! Like, like someone's playing some mad joke on me?! Putting me in this body when/

MISS LILLIAN. hey! I love this body I love you.

*(**JACK** smiles. She blushes.)*

Well, I/

JACK. I love you.

MISS LILLIAN. .

JACK. .

MISS LILLIAN. .

JACK. Fuck!

MISS LILLIAN. Fuck!

(They laugh.)

JACK & MISS LILLIAN. I love you!

JACK. I love you/

MISS LILLIAN. I love you/

JACK & MISS LILLIAN. I love you!

*(They kiss then **MISS LILLIAN** suddenly pulls away and starts pacing the room.)*

MISS LILLIAN. It's *not* fair!

JACK. *(Laughs.)* I know!

MISS LILLIAN. Not fucking fair!

JACK. I know! You're beautiful, I love you/

MISS LILLIAN. I love *you!* I *Love* you! And I *want* your *child!*

JACK. Well, I can't do much 'bout/

MISS LILLIAN. no *I know!* I, I'm not saying it's your/

JACK. I *want* to! And sometimes it feels like I could/

MISS LILLIAN. I know!

JACK. It's so intense/

MISS LILLIAN. *so* intense! Sometimes you just *look* at me and I'm sure I'm pregnant!

JACK. Hahaha!

MISS LILLIAN. No but seriously Jack! This, *energy* between us? It's *powerful!* It's god given I'm sure/

JACK. oh, please don't/

MISS LILLIAN. no really! If god is good. Then this is god. Because *this?* Is good.

JACK. This is good!

MISS LILLIAN. This is good.

(They kiss. She pulls away, full of fire for her ideas.)

This energy has got to *go* somewhere? Surely?! Make something?

JACK. Yes!

MISS LILLIAN. It can't just, disappear?! Something *this good?*

JACK. I know! Sometimes, when you cry out/

MISS LILLIAN. oh god/

JACK. no I love it/

MISS LILLIAN. really/

JACK. I *love* it! And when you moan?

MISS LILLIAN. Oh god/

JACK. and your *whole body shakes!?!* And this *noise* comes out of you and?! And then *my* body, *goes* it just *goes* and it's like /.. And I'm certain, *completely* certain, that we just made a new star burst up in the sky! Or, or a mountain fall down, somewhere?! Or a flower, push open and bloom! Somewhere in the world, we just made something *bloom*! I'm sure of it!

MISS LILLIAN. You're funny.

JACK. Yeah?

MISS LILLIAN. Yeah.

JACK. Funny lookin'?

MISS LILLIAN. That too.

(She kisses them. Blackout.)

(Lights up. They're fast asleep, on a nest of towels on the floor next to the bath, holding each other. It's soft and beautiful. Blackout.)

(Lights up. **JACK** *asleep.* **LILLIAN** *shakes* **JACK** *awake.* **JACK***'s groggy but still fast to reach for their gun.)*

JACK. What's wrong?!

MISS LILLIAN. Nothing! I need to speak to you!

JACK. Fucksake! I thought there was/

MISS LILLIAN. no! No, it's fine!

JACK. Don't *do* that!

MISS LILLIAN. I need to *speak* to you!

JACK. OK?!

MISS LILLIAN. I think I'm pregnant!

JACK. *(Laughs.)* What?!

MISS LILLIAN. No, really! I can *feel* it. Your seed inside me.

JACK. Mmm! Say that again!

(They kiss. It gets hot, fast. **JACK** *pulls away.)*

Fuck! You're killin' me!

MISS LILLIAN. Then you'll die a happy guy?

JACK. The happiest.

MISS LILLIAN. What'll we call the baby?

JACK. I dunno.

*(***JACK** *lights a cigarette.)*

MISS LILLIAN. Come on!

JACK. Is it a boy or a girl?

MISS LILLIAN. As if that matters.

JACK. No?

MISS LILLIAN. Course not!

JACK. Seems to matter quite a lot/

MISS LILLIAN. but not to us! *Our* baby? They can be whoever they are! We'll give them a name that's good for either, both, anything! And they can wear whatever they want, and/

JACK. it's not as easy as you/

MISS LILLIAN. I know/

JACK. no, it's not just *clothes* it's/

MISS LILLIAN. I know/

JACK. no you don't! You don't get it! I'm sorry but, you don't.

MISS LILLIAN. Don't what?

JACK. Look, people aren't kind. Not always/

MISS LILLIAN. so/

JACK. they'll be saying all sorts of shit/

MISS LILLIAN. I don't care!

JACK. You will! You'll be laughed at/

MISS LILLIAN. let 'em laugh! I literally don't care. I'm just gonna do what's right for us, for our family/

JACK. I don't get a family.

MISS LILLIAN. What?

JACK. *(Turning away.)* Nothin'.

MISS LILLIAN. *(Fierce with love.)* Hey! Hey?! You do. With me.

JACK. .

MISS LILLIAN. *(Fierce with love.)* Alright?

JACK. Alright.

MISS LILLIAN. Good.

(They hold each other, tight.)

Would you prefer a son?

JACK. A moon.

*(**JACK** kisses her belly and rests their head there. She strokes his hair. Blackout.)*

*(Lights up. **MISS LILLIAN** is asleep, and pregnant. **JACK** is holding her, humming softly. Full lights fade up to daytime as **JACK** sings a snippet of a song, and the blue neon fades away. **JACK** slips out of the towel nest without waking **MISS LILLIAN** and heads to the bar. **JACK** lights a cigarette and makes coffee. **MISS LILLIAN** wakes.)*

MISS LILLIAN. Jack?

JACK. *(To us.)* I love how she calls my name.

MISS LILLIAN. Jack?!

*(**JACK** enjoys the sound, dancing and smoking. **MISS LILLIAN** dances in the towel nest, sleepy and smiley. **JACK** returns with mugs of tea and a newspaper. **MISS LILLIAN** smiles at **JACK** then stops at the sight of us.)*

(To us.) Oh! We were just /..

JACK. .

MISS LILLIAN. *(To us.)* Never mind.

*(**MISS LILLIAN** pulls **JACK** down to her and wraps herself around him. They share tea, cigarettes and the newspaper. They enjoy their version of domestic bliss, on a nest of towels, next to a neon blue bath.)*

Scene Twelve

*(***MARY*** enters. She's shocked by the state of the room, and the sight of the couple.)*

MISS LILLIAN. *(Big smile.)* Mary! Come on in!

MARY. Well!

*(***MISS LILLIAN*** stands and* **MARY** *sees that she is pregnant. She stares. They celebrate like squealing sisters.)*

MISS LILLIAN. I'll get you some coffee.

*(***KID*** runs in and jumps on* **JACK.***)*

KID. I got you!

JACK. Sure did! Good ambush kiddo!

*(***KID*** suddenly spots* **MISS LILLIAN***'s belly.)*

KID. Woah! What's that?!

JACK. It's, a baby, it's gonna be a/

KID. how'd that happen?!

MARY. Kid!

JACK. Oh! Well, erm /.. You see, when two people/

MARY. he knows how babies are made. He's asking how *you* made/

JACK. oh/

MARY. which is *very* rude!

JACK. Oh, no it's OK! We erm/

KID. magic?

JACK. Yeah. Yeah, magic.

KID. Woah!

JACK. Yeah. *(Looking at* **MISS LILLIAN.***)* Woah.

*(***MISS LILLIAN** *smiles at* **JACK.***)*

MISS LILLIAN. Hey Kid, I'm gonna make your mama some pancakes, you want some?

KID. Yeah!

MISS LILLIAN. Wanna help me make 'em?

KID. Can I mama?

MARY. Sure.

*(***KID** *celebrates and exits with* **MISS LILLIAN.***)*

JACK. Good mornin'!

MARY. *(Eyebrows raised.)* Sure is... So I guess you're staying? Not chasing revenge. Not fighting off bandits. You're hanging up your guns, and you're/

JACK. guess so!

MARY. You'd better *know* so! Cus she's the best of 'em! She's/

JACK. I know/

MARY. you'd better!

*(***MISS LILLIAN** *enters.)*

MISS LILLIAN. Jack honey, can you get us some eggs? Chickens should have laid some by now.

JACK. Sure! I love you.

MISS LILLIAN. I love you too.

*(***MISS LILLIAN** *exits.)*

MARY. If I hear, one word, that you/

*(**MISS LILLIAN** sprints in and kisses **JACK**, and then runs back out again.)*

MISS LILLIAN. *(Running out.)* Sorry I just had to!

*(**JACK** beams and blushes. **MARY** stares.)*

JACK. I love her.

MARY. .

JACK. I'm staying.

*(**MARY** stares at **JACK**, unrelenting. Cracks start to appear in **JACK**.)*

I /.. Look, I never planned this/

MARY. none of us do.

JACK. I didn't even know this could be *possible* for me! And now it's here I /..

MARY. What? You what?

*(**KID** runs in covered in flour.)*

KID. Jack, where's the eggs?

JACK. Coming.

KID. Quick!

*(**KID** runs out. **JACK** suddenly panics. **MARY** stares.)*

MARY. Look, I never wanted children. Never seen myself as a mother, never wanted never, *felt,* that *thing*. Whatever *that thing* is you're meant to have, I /.. But my husband always wanted babies. Seven, he said. *Seven?!* Oh god I loved him! Love, like /.. But then he's gone. And I'm left with Kid. And look, I sure ain't perfect but, well he's alive and half decent and I reckons if I can do it then you can/

JACK. Don't think I can/

MARY. Why/

JACK. I don't, I, I'm not/

MARY. what/

JACK. good! I ain't no good.

MARY. You are! Oh honey you are!

JACK. .

MARY. I seen you, out playin' with Kid. *Hours* of it?! Put me to shame. Ain't been much playin' in our house, it's true. I ain't felt like I could find the time to spare but/ You should know my housework's piling up and the to-do list is longer than ever. But we been playin' all mornin', all mornin' long.

KID. *(Off stage.)* Jack!

MARY. He loves you. Cus you're good.

JACK. *(To themselves.)* A good bad guy?

KID. *(Off stage.)* Jack!

JACK. *(To* **KID.***)* Coming! *(To* **MARY.***)* I'm staying.

MARY. You'd better be.

JACK. I am. I'm staying.

MISS LILLIAN & KID. *(Off stage.)* Jack?!

*(**JACK** goes to leave but **MARY** beats him to it.)*

MARY. I'll get 'em. You stay if you're stayin'.

*(**MARY** exits. **JACK** stands still, thinking, feeling the enormity of it all. He turns to us.)*

Scene Thirteen

*(**JACK** suddenly stretches. They smile. They dance, for themself, then for us. **JACK** points to the band and they begin playing. He conducts the lights to change and we see that the saloon has been transformed into a cabaret dream. **JACK** drags the bathtub offstage and returns to dance, enjoying the band. **JAYNE** and **LOU** enter, hand in hand, a happy couple. **JACK** conducts and they join in with the song. **SALLY ANN** enters with **MARY**, then **MISS LILLIAN**. More are introduced to the song. **KID** enters and dances. They all sing together, looking out to us as other townspeople, no fourth wall, all united. Suddenly **SHERIFF JONES** appears, in full drag, and brings the house down. It's fabulous. Everyone is their most free, open and joyful self. It's queertopia.)*

MARY. Sheriff Jones! You are fabulous!

SHERIFF. Why thank you!

SALLY ANN. Oh, my, goodness?!

LOU. Ignore her. You look amazing!

JAYNE. Shots!

*(**JAYNE** appears with a tray of shots, and a glass of water for the **SHERIFF**. They all raise a glass.)*

(To us.) What'll we toast to?

LOU. To love!

JAYNE. Oh! You're sweet! Come 'ere!

*(**JAYNE** kisses **LOU.** **MARY** wolf whistles and the **SHERIFF** laughs. Everyone but **SALLY ANN** is happy for the couple.)*

SALLY ANN. I didn't see that!

LOU. Well let us do it again for you!

*(**LOU** kisses **JAYNE** defiantly. **SALLY ANN** can't look.)*

SALLY ANN. *(To us.)* This whole town has gone crazy!

*(**MARY** marches over to **SALLY ANN**, fierce with love. **MARY** hands her a shot of liquor.)*

MARY. Walk in the spirit Sally Ann.

*(**SALLY ANN** hesitates, looking at us, then takes the shot. **MARY** raises her glass.)*

To love?

SHERIFF. *(To us.)* To freedom!

LOU. Yes!

EVERYONE. To freedom!

MARY. *(To **SHERIFF.**)* I'm proud of you.

SHERIFF. Thank you.

JAYNE. *(Too loud.)* Yeah Sheriff. You look really well.

*(The **SHERIFF** suddenly looks shy. **MISS LILLIAN** senses it.)*

MISS LILLIAN. I love your dress.

SHERIFF. It's silk!

MISS LILLIAN. Ooh!

*(The **SHERIFF** twirls. **JAYNE** dances with him. **SALLY ANN** is appalled. **MARY** glares at her.)*

SALLY ANN. *(To herself.)* Love is a gift from god. Love is a *gift*, from god. Love is a/

*(**SALLY ANN** looks at **JACK** who winks. **SALLY ANN** takes a deep breath and turns to **JAYNE**.)*

Jayne?

JAYNE. Sally Ann?

SALLY ANN. Will you show me that dance move you just did? I'd love to learn it.

*(**JAYNE** hesitates then shows her. **SALLY ANN** stumbles through an attempt. **JAYNE** laughs. They try again and crack up laughing.)*

*(**MISS LILLIAN** kisses **JACK** and twirls around.)*

MISS LILLIAN. Oh god I'm so happy I could burst!

MARY. Not yet! You've got a few more months yet!

JACK. Yes, stay in there little one!

MISS LILLIAN. OK yes, but really, I didn't know I could feel this happy!

MARY. Same.

JAYNE. Same!

MISS LILLIAN. All that time, trying, to feel /.. And pretending, and /..

MARY. Oh honey!

MISS LILLIAN. I just didn't know!

*(Everyone nods at her kindly. **JACK** holds her hand.)*

Oh god, why am I so emotional?! Must be the hormones/

MARY. because it's fucking revolutionary!

JAYNE. Yes!

MARY. We all deserve love.

KID. Me too?

MARY. Especially you baby. You're the best of them all.

*(**KID** does a celebration dance. Everyone laughs and joins in. **MARY** and **MISS LILLIAN** dance together. The **SHERIFF** gets swept up in the joy and dances on the bar.)*

SHERIFF. Oh! I feel *fantastic!*

JAYNE. You look it!

SHERIFF. I am a man, who feels sexy in silk?!

MISS LILLIAN & MARY. Yes!

SHERIFF. For too long I have denied myself this. Well, no more! From now on I will enjoy, every, single, inch of it!

EVERYONE. Yes!

*(The **SHERIFF** dances and sings again. Everyone joins in with the number, growing in confidence. It's vibrant and joyous. Suddenly the music warps into something contemporary. Deep bass makes our bodies buzz, and the lights change to shift us somewhere else. The dance becomes more abstract, more animal and raw, as they all wonder at what their own bodies can do, at the power that's coursing through them just under their skin. The whole town has defrosted and they can move their bodies freely. There's nothing but delight and desire. Then suddenly the lights snap back to normal and everyone bursts into the chorus*

together, enjoying the whole space, wild and raucous. The audience is encouraged to join in, the whole space bursting with joy. Just as it all reaches its peak the doors suddenly bang open. A group of men enter. Everyone is stunned. Blackout.)

Interval

ACT TWO

Masc Off/Mask Off

(Loud music. A reprise of the song from before, an explosion of joy and delight. The men enter and watch. Lights and sound morph as time blurs. They all squirm in shame, pulling at their own skin, silently screaming. Then we suddenly snap back to reality. Silence and stillness.)

FRANK. Well! That ain't quite the welcome home we was expecting!

(Everyone bursts into life. **SALLY ANN** *screams and runs into the arms of her husband* **JOHN. JAYNE** *quickly jumps off* **LOU**'*s lap and runs into the arms of her fiancé* **JAMES.** *The* **SHERIFF** *tries to be braver than he feels.* **MISS LILLIAN** *freezes, caught in a nightmare, unable to look at* **JACK** *who's sat beside her waiting for her cue.* **LOU** *stands shyly as their husband* **GEORGE** *walks towards them, staring, arms outreached.)*

GEORGE. Lucy?

LOU. .

KID. Their name's Lou. That's how they dress now/

MARY. Kid!

*(**MARY** pulls **KID** away. **GEORGE** stares at **LOU**, who burns with shame. **GEORGE** laughs, nervous, aware everyone is watching.)*

GEORGE. What's all this?! You playin' dress up?

JAMES. They must be! Look at this!

*(**JAMES** points at the **SHERIFF**. The men laugh. The **SHERIFF** stares at the floor.)*

FRANK. Well I'll be! Sheriff?! That really you?!

SHERIFF. .

JAMES. Sure is!

JOHN. What's the big idea Sheriff?!

JAMES. You all gone *crazy* without us?!

GEORGE. Must have! *(Laughing at **LOU**, unsure and embarrassed.)* State of you?!

*(**MARY** is suddenly in **GEORGE**'s face.)*

MARY. We don't disrespect each other round here.

GEORGE. *(Laughs.)* That right?

MARY. *(Stern.)* That's right.

KID. Yeah!

GEORGE. *(Laughs.)* Well OK then, little lady!

MARY. Who you calling little?

GEORGE. *(Laughs.)* Woah!

FRANK. Hey now?! Ain't no need for things to go sideways!

GEORGE. No there ain't!

FRANK. Hell we only just got back?!

JAMES. Yeah! Shouldn't we be having a party?!

JOHN. I'd say so!

*(**JOHN** spins **SALLY ANN** around who squeals. **LOU** won't look at **GEORGE**, who's embarrassed and trying not to be. **JAMES** tries to dance with **JAYNE** but she's not in the mood.)*

JAMES. Or not?

*(**MARY** is staring at **FRANK**, totally deadpan. He's uncomfortable under her gaze.)*

FRANK. Howdie, Mary.

*(**MARY** stares. **FRANK** pulls a face at the men, who laugh with him.)*

*(To **MARY**.)* Well, hell, you ain't changed a bit.

KID. You ain't neither!

*(The men laugh at **FRANK**. **FRANK** is embarrassed and tries to ruffle **KID**'s hair but is too slow to catch him. **MARY** doesn't flinch, staring at **FRANK**. **FRANK** can't bear her gaze.)*

FRANK. Where's my wife at?! Eh? Where is she?!

*(**JACK** looks at **MISS LILLIAN**. She can't look back.)*

MISS LILLIAN. I'm here.

*(**MISS LILLIAN** stands, revealing the baby bump. Everyone stares at **FRANK**.)*

FRANK. Pregnant?!

(No one breathes.)

My wife? My /..

*(**MISS LILLIAN** carefully approaches **FRANK**. Everyone watches, still not breathing. **MISS LILLIAN** lays **FRANK**'s hand on her belly.)*

MISS LILLIAN. Yes Frank. We're pregnant.

*(Sudden magic moment of suspension – everyone is looking at **MISS LILLIAN** and **FRANK**. **JACK** stands slowly, puts on their hat and walks through the bar. The women, **KID**, the **SHERIFF** and **LOU** all look at **JACK** as he passes them. **JACK** stops in front of **MISS LILLIAN**, but she can't look at him. **JACK** waits, then steps away. At the last second **MISS LILLIAN** changes her mind, she reaches out for **JACK**, but too late. **JACK** disappears. Everyone feels it. **FRANK** spins, confused.)*

FRANK. A baby! We're having a baby! Someone get us a drink!

*(The men all cheer and bottles are opened. **GEORGE** sulks by the bar, staring at **LOU**. Everyone sneaks private looks at each other behind **FRANK**'s back. **KID** looks for **JACK**.)*

KID. Mama?

MARY. Shush now, come here to me.

*(**MISS LILLIAN** and **MARY** stare at each other, a silent conversation. **FRANK** doesn't notice, spinning from the news.)*

FRANK. My beautiful wife, lemme look at you!

*(**FRANK** hugs and kisses **MISS LILLIAN**, his hands all over her. She doesn't respond, still staring at **MARY**.)*

KID. But mama/

MARY. shush!

FRANK. A baby?! Sweet miracle! Oh god I missed you!

MISS LILLIAN. .

FRANK. What's wrong honey? You ain't acting/

MISS LILLIAN. we thought you were dead!

FRANK. What?

MISS LILLIAN. We all thought/

FRANK. no! Not us, not yet!

SALLY ANN. We hadn't heard from you in such a long time!

JAMES. You didn't get our letters?

JAYNE. No!

SALLY ANN. No! Not one!

JAMES. We sent hundreds!

JOHN. Well, not *hundreds!*

JAMES. I did!

JOHN. You liar!

JAMES. I sent you loads Miss Jayne. As neat as I could, with my best hand/

SALLY ANN. we never received *one!* Not even one!

JOHN. How queer! They can't have all got lost in the mail?

JAYNE. Nothing ever arrives in this fucking town!

JAMES. Jayne?!

SALLY ANN. I never received *one!* For *months!*

JOHN. Gee honey! Did you think I'd run off and left you?

SALLY ANN. Well I, not quite that, I/

JOHN. you did! Thought I'd deserted you?!

SALLY ANN. We thought all kinds of things! We all did!

JAYNE. Especially after we heard about the explosion.

JOHN. At Silverton? We heard about that too. Gee, it's awful sad.

SALLY ANN. We thought you were there! Trapped under ground!

JOHN. No honey!

JAMES. We'd moved on from Silverton weeks before that!

SALLY ANN. We thought you were dead!

*(**SALLY ANN** bursts into tears and **JOHN** holds her. **JAYNE** doesn't cry, but **JAMES** hugs her anyway. **MARY** holds **KID** tight, whilst staring at **MISS LILLIAN**. **FRANK** squeezes **MISS LILLIAN**'s shoulder, but she barely notices, staring back at **MARY**. **KID** watches everyone, confused. **JAYNE** stares at the floor, telepathically connected to **LOU** across the room. **GEORGE** stares at **LOU**, who doesn't move towards him, can't barely look at him. Everyone glances at **GEORGE** and **LOU**, the only couple not together.)*

FRANK. Well, we ain't! Ain't deserted nor dead, and that's worth celebrating!

*(**FRANK** raises a glass. All the men copy.)*

To not being dead!

FRANK, JAMES, JOHN & GEORGE. To not being dead!

*(They all down a shot and immediately pour another. The wives all sneak looks at each other. **FRANK** pulls **MISS LILLIAN** down to sit on his lap, and she complies. **FRANK** rubs his*

hands over her belly and kisses her cheek. He whispers in her ear. She smiles, but holds her breath. **MARY** *stares at* **MISS LILLIAN**, *who can't look back.* **JAYNE** *pours herself a large whiskey and downs it.* **JAMES** *is shocked.* **SALLY ANN** *is horrified.)*

JAMES. Hey! Since when do you drink whiskey?

JAYNE. *(Shrugs.)* Lot's changed since you been away.

JAMES. That right?

(**JAYNE** *pours another.* **JOHN** *tuts and* **SALLY ANN** *copies him.)*

SALLY ANN. Goodness! So unbecoming!

JAYNE. Oh you was drinking it yourself barely five minutes ago?!

SALLY ANN. I wasn't!

JAYNE. Don't start playing the good girl now just cus he's back!

(**JAYNE** *downs more whiskey,* **JAMES** *is shocked.* **SALLY ANN** *starts praying fervently.)*

SALLY ANN. God please help change Jayne's heart, please help her, oh Lord/

JAYNE. hey hey hey! None of that nonsense for me please!

SALLY ANN. Oh Lord, save her soul/

JAYNE. no Lord, don't be saving my nothin'!

MISS LILLIAN. Jayne!

JAYNE. I've watched you torture our Mary with it/

MARY. Jayne/

JAYNE. always tryna save her soul?! When her soul's doing just fine, thank you very much!

MARY. Jayne, I really don't need/

SALLY ANN. oh Lord, I pray you help change Jayne's heart/

JAYNE. you keep your prayers to yourself Sally Ann, or you'll lose your teeth you hear me?!

JAMES. Jayne!

JAYNE. Oh hush!

*(***JAYNE*** shrugs* **JAMES** *away. The men are stunned.)*

FRANK. Well hell! Don't stop 'em now, they're just gettin' started!

JAMES. I'm awful sorry John.

JOHN. That's quite alright.

JAYNE. What you apologising to *him* for?!

JAMES. I dunno quite what's got into her.

JAYNE. Helloooo?!

JAMES. Hell, I need a drink.

JOHN. Me too!

GEORGE. And me.

FRANK. Well pour 'em up lads! Let's all have one!

JOHN. Yes! And pour one for the Sheriff here!

FRANK. Yes, and get him out that goddamn dress!

(The men laugh. **JOHN** *bows elaborately, teasing the* **SHERIFF**. *The* **SHERIFF** *tries to hold onto his dignity.)*

JOHN. Well now, Miss Sheriff, what'll it be? Tequila to match them petticoats?

SHERIFF. I don't drink no more.

JOHN. *(Laughing.)* Sure! And birds don't fly!

FRANK. *(Laughing.)* Get the man a drink!

KID. No!

GEORGE. If he is still a man?

JAMES. *(Laughing.)* Yeah unless his cock's dropped off?!

Hey Sheriff! You still got a cock under that dress?

(The men laugh harder. The **SHERIFF** *burns.)*

MARY. Hey, stop that.

FRANK. *(Laughing.)* Oh get him a drink!

JAMES. *(Laughing.)* And some trousers!

JOHN. *(Laughing.)* He can have hers! George's wife's got a pretty pair on!

GEORGE. *(Laughing.)* Oh that ain't my wife! My wife wouldn't shame me like that.

JOHN. *(Laughing.)* Oh they suit her!

JAMES. *(Laughing.)* Sure do!

JOHN. *(Laughing.)* She always was a *handsome* kinda gal!

SALLY ANN. John!

JAMES. *(Laughing.)* Handsome!

JOHN. What? She is!

FRANK. *(Laughing.)* Yeah but Sheriff ain't that pretty?

JAMES. *(Laughing.)* Sure ain't!

GEORGE. Come 'ere Sheriff, lemme fix you a drink.

SHERIFF. No, I told you, I don't/

*(**GEORGE** pours a drink over the **SHERIFF**'s head. The men gasp then crack up. The women stare.)*

GEORGE. There! Now you've had your drink, let's see what you got under here!

*(**GEORGE** grabs at the **SHERIFF**'s dress, trying to lift it. The men laugh as the **SHERIFF** struggles. The women look away. **KID** tries to stop **GEORGE** but isn't strong enough. **MARY** can't bear it and tries to stop **GEORGE**.)*

KID. No no no! Stop it!

MARY. What in the hell? Stop that! Stop it!

*(**GEORGE** tries to resist **MARY**, and **KID**. He accidentally knocks **MARY** back. He goes to apologise but **LOU** is suddenly there, and punches **GEORGE**, bang on the nose. **GEORGE** is mortified.)*

GEORGE. What the hell?!

*(A scrappy fight breaks out between **GEORGE** and **LOU**. The men break it up. The **SHERIFF** pushes **LOU** out the doors and follows them.)*

Yeah go on go! Go swap your goddamn clothes! And bring my wife back in here! When she's dressed like a goddamn woman goddammit!

*(**GEORGE** tries to laugh it off to the other men, but he's full of shame and rage. **GEORGE** starts to rearrange the furniture. **JAMES** joins him. **KID** tries to stop them. The women still can't look at each other.)*

KID. No, leave it!

FRANK. Now now, let's get this place tidied up a little!

MARY. Don't touch him!

FRANK. Well now. I think that's quite enough!

JOHN. Can say that again!

FRANK. Come on now, clean yourselves up.

*(***MISS LILLIAN, JAYNE** *and* **SALLY ANN** *walk to the mirror. They wipe away any signs of expression. They daren't make eye contact with each other, daren't witness the shrinking.* **MARY** *glares at them, disgusted.* **KID** *also can't believe it.)*

KID. Mama?!

MARY. Let's go Kid.

*(***MARY** *grabs* **KID** *by the hand and marches out with him.* **MISS LILLIAN** *goes to stop* **MARY** *on the way out, but can't bring herself to do it.)*

FRANK. Well, thank god for that! She always was a party pooper!

(The men chuckle. The women stare at the floor, ashamed.)

God I love this place! Built this bar with my very own hands.

JOHN. Sure got the scars to prove it!

FRANK. Sure do!

JAMES. I pain'ted those walls.

JOHN. I varnished this floor.

FRANK. My wife made those curtains.

GEORGE. Mine too.

*(**GEORGE** downs some whiskey, angry and hurting. **FRANK** slaps a hand on his back. He pours them both a shot.)*

FRANK. We fought together. We built this town, together.

*(They down a shot each. Then **FRANK** pours more for everyone else.)*

To home!

EVERYONE. To home!

(Everyone drinks.)

JAMES. Gee, it sure is good to be back. Feels like we've been to the moon!

JOHN. Can say that again!

SALLY ANN. What's it like out there honey?

GEORGE. Same as here!

JOHN. Gee some things are different!

SALLY ANN. Like what?

JAMES. The water don't taste the same.

JAYNE. The water?!

FRANK. *(Laughing.)* Oh shut up!

JOHN. *(Laughing.)* You dummy!

JAMES. It don't!

FRANK. *(Laughing.)* On and on about the water/

JAMES. I'm telling ya it don't/

JOHN. *(Laughing.)* sure sure!

SALLY ANN. Well now, what else?

JOHN. What else what?

SALLY ANN. Well.

*(**MISS LILLIAN** and **JAYNE** silently urge **SALLY ANN** on.)*

Well now, in truth honey, what we *all* want to know, and without sounding too forward I /.. Well I guess it's true that circumstances do force a woman to sound a little, *forward* sometimes, and I, of course I wouldn't mean to/

JOHN. you go on ahead and say it honey! Whatever it is, you say it plain and simple for us. We won't be offended, will we boys?

JAMES. Depends on what it is.

JOHN. *(To **JAMES**.)* Oh hush! *(To **SALLY ANN**.)* Go on honey.

SALLY ANN. Well, what we *all* want to know, *need* to really because, because well you see our supplies are getting so low and, you coming back *now* is, well it's just a *miracle* really, not least because we /.. And you're /.. And so *now* we, really do, *need* to know/

JAYNE. where's the gold?

SALLY ANN. Jayne!

JAYNE. Well we'd have been here all day if you'd/

SALLY ANN. there are ways and means Miss Jayne!

JOHN. Well I'll be! You kinda knocked me sideways a little/

SALLY ANN. I'm sorry honey, I didn't mean/

JOHN. no it's OK! It's, it's just /.. Well now, you see /.. The truth is/

GEORGE. we ain't got no gold.

(Silence.)

SALLY ANN. *(Quietly.)* What?

JAMES. We ain't/

JAYNE. but you been gone *months?! (To* **FRANK.***)* You said you'd find Gold. You said it was a sure thing!

FRANK. Well now/

JAMES. We worked *hard!* To the bone!

JAYNE. I don't doubt it!

SALLY ANN. None of us do!

JAMES. And little Gold we found, we ate/

GEORGE. and we barely ate.

(Silence.)

JOHN. I'm sorry honey/

SALLY ANN. no/

JOHN. we tried, mighty hard/

SALLY ANN. no stop, stop it! I know you did, I know!

(The men are ashamed.)

Now, have no fear. The good Lord will provide.

JAYNE. Well he better hurry up.

SALLY ANN. Jayne!

JAYNE. I'm just sayin'!

JOHN. Well it didn't help that there was all those Immigrants there too!

FRANK. John. Come on now, you know my rules!

JAMES. Yeah! Italians, Poles, Greeks! Taking our jobs! And our gold, and/

JAYNE. James?!

JAMES. What? It's true!

JAYNE. You ain't never talked like that before?!

JAMES. Well you ain't seen it! I have!

FRANK. OK, that's enough of/

JOHN. he's right/

FRANK. John/

JOHN. now look I'm all for emancipation, I truly am, but/

GEORGE. but what?

JOHN. But it made the queue longer. That's all I'm saying.

FRANK. Well good cus that's plenty! Come on now?! Look here, we been away, nearly a whole year! Missing on each other and, well, going half crazy it seems wanting to be back home! To *our town!* Our little island, away from the world and all it's /.. What we've built here? It's precious! It's *ours!* And that's something to be proud of!

JOHN. Damn straight!

FRANK. So let's not get to bickering over things that, really ain't worth the time of day. We're *home*! Hell we should be celebrating!

JAMES. Yeah!

FRANK. Cus after all, we're a family! Ain't no time apart can change that.

SALLY ANN. Amen!

FRANK. We're family! And we're *home* goddammit! So pour 'em up! And play it loud boys!

> *(The band starts playing. The husbands dance with their wives. It's square. The women steal glances at each other, maybe sneak a moment of true expression, then go back to playing their role.* **MISS LILLIAN** *looks depressed. The* **SHERIFF** *and* **LOU** *slip into place, back in their original costume.* **JAYNE** *tries not to look at* **LOU.**

The **SHERIFF** *tries not to drink.* **LOU** *dances with their husband, it's painfully awkward. Everyone is trying their best.)*

(The world spirals as we jump forward in time.)

Scene Two

*(***FRANK*** is holding court for the husbands who sit laughing with their wives on their laps or stood nearby.* **GEORGE** *is standing alone at the bar, drinking and hurting.* **LOU** *is stealing glances at him, and trying not to watch* **JAMES** *touching* **JAYNE**. *The piano tinkles politely in the background.* **FRANK**'*s a bit drunk and a bit too loud.* **MISS LILLIAN** *is embarrassed.)*

FRANK. So there I am, a whole bag of nerves! I've been planning this for *weeks*, tryna muster up the courage, and find the right time, and I'm *sure*, that *today* is the day! So, I got the ring in my pocket/

JOHN. ah bless ya/

FRANK. and I've got the words going round 'n' round my head/

JOHN. I know it/

FRANK. and I'm about *just* right and ready...when she bursts in from the store room and goes "*Frank, I been thinking 'bout the insurance, and it's plenty cheaper if we're married, so how's about it?!*"

(The men laugh loudly. **GEORGE** *stares at his drink. The women smile politely.* **MISS LILLIAN** *burns.)*

Ain't that right honey?

MISS LILLIAN. .

FRANK. I said ain't that right?

MISS LILLIAN. *(Quietly.)* That's right.

FRANK. You've gone all shy!

MISS LILLIAN. No.

FRANK. You have! What've you gone all shy for?!

*(**FRANK** tickles her and she squirms away from him.)*

JAMES. Sure is a beautiful thing when a man finds a good wife.

FRANK. Amen to that!

(The women bristle.)

JAMES. I just can't wait to marry my Jayne. You know we're childhood sweethearts?

GEORGE. We know.

JAMES. Been destined to get married since we was knee high, ain't we? Oh yeah, she's a good woman, keeps a good home, don't ya honey?

JAYNE. Good?

JAMES. Well OK, more than good! You fishin' for compliments there sweetheart?

JAYNE. No, no I/

JAMES. nah I know I know! I'm just teasing ya a little!

*(**JAYNE** and **LOU** clock eyes, then look away quickly. **JAMES** sees it, but thinks nothing of it.)*

JOHN. Marriage is a blessing, it's true. I ain't even half the man I am today without my Sally Ann. She sure is a good woman.

SALLY ANN. Why, thank you honey!

JOHN. It's true! We don't deserve you. We sure are blessed ain't we gentlemen?!

JAMES. Sure are!

JOHN. To good women!

(The men raise a glass. **GEORGE** *stares at his shoes. The wives can't look at each other.)*

FRANK, JAMES, JOHN & GEORGE. To good women!

(The men drink. **GEORGE** *burns.)*

FRANK. Good women? Well now, I dunno 'bout that! Mine's fine, I guess.

*(***FRANK** *tickles* **MISS LILLIAN**, *she squirms.)*

Nah I'm just messing! She's fine, she's mighty fine!

*(***FRANK** *tickles her and kisses her neck. She shoves him, harder than she meant to, he almost topples off his stool.)*

Jesus woman!

MISS LILLIAN. I'm sorry I/

FRANK. you got muscles all of a sudden? Did I marry a man and not know it?!

JAMES. Wouldn't be the only one!

*(***GEORGE** *explodes. Volcanic, and eager to fight.* **FRANK, JOHN** *and the* **SHERIFF** *restrain him.* **SALLY ANN** *is horrified.)*

GEORGE. TELL HIM TO KEEP HIS FUCKING MOUTH SHUT!

FRANK. ALRIGHT ALRIGHT!

SHERIFF. CALM DOWN!

GEORGE. GET OFF ME!

SHERIFF. CALM *DOWN!*

JOHN. HEY NOW! CALM YOURSELF!

GEORGE. GET OFF ME!

SHERIFF. GEORGE!

GEORGE. GET THE *FUCK* OFF ME!

FRANK. ENOUGH! THAT'S *ENOUGH!*

(The men pant as the dust settles. **GEORGE** *is pinned and held by the men. They breathe together. It's tender and strong.* **GEORGE** *nods.)*

GEORGE. *(Quietly.)* You can let go.

(They let go of **GEORGE**, *who looks at everyone. The women look scared.)*

Yeah, well, it scares me too... It does!... A man can keep it down most of the time, but when it comes up? /.. It's kinda frightening, truth be told.

FRANK. Well now/

GEORGE. where do we put it? Honestly? Where's it all meant to go?

(Everyone stares at **GEORGE**. *He's surprised himself.* **FRANK** *dives into laughter.)*

FRANK. Well now! Thanks for sharing there Sunbeam!

JAMES. Ha! Yeah, gee thanks!

FRANK. Though I *think* that's the whiskey talking to be quite honest/

GEORGE. who you calling sunbeam?

FRANK. You! Spilling your mouth like that?

SHERIFF. Alright alright/

JAMES. yeah what's come over you? I was only messin'/

GEORGE. I dunno! I dunno/

SHERIFF. settle down/

FRANK. this is a goddamn bar! Ain't no pillowtalk in a bar!

JOHN. Hah! Exactly!

FRANK. Save that for your wife's ear if you must/

GEORGE. oh she ain't listening!

JOHN. Well good! Seems she's got some sense after all!

(The men laugh. **GEORGE** *stares, sways.* **FRANK** *smiles, amused.)*

FRANK. Sit down sunbeam.

*(***GEORGE** *leans on the bar, his back to everyone.* **FRANK** *laughs.* **MISS LILLIAN** *can't bear it.)*

Sulking little/

MISS LILLIAN. Frank! Don't!

FRANK. What?

MISS LILLIAN. Just, leave the man be!

FRANK. Hell woman, he don't need your interfering! What'd you know about anythin'?

*(***FRANK** *laughs.* **MISS LILLIAN** *looks at him like she's seeing him new. She stands and walks away from the table. He performs for the lads a "oh I'm in trouble" routine and crosses the room to her.)*

Ah gee! I'm sorry I upset ya. Come here.

(She doesn't move.)

(Lightly.) Come here!

(She doesn't move. **FRANK** *feels everyone looking.)*

Lillian.

(She doesn't move. **FRANK** *laughs, embarrassed. He suddenly moves towards* **MISS LILLIAN**. *Everyone holds their breath.* **FRANK** *kisses* **MISS LILLIAN**, *hard. She freezes but he doesn't seem to notice. The* **SHERIFF** *steps forward but does nothing.* **FRANK** *holds* **MISS LILLIAN**'*s face in his hand.)*

There she is.

*(***FRANK** *smacks her bum, hard, and turns to the room watching him.)*

Where's the music at?! We was having a celebration here, wasn't we?! Wasn't we?!

JOHN. Sure was Frank/

FRANK. well then, get up and dance! Come on now! Guys and gals together! Dancing! Like the good ole days! That's right, that's right!

(The band starts. The men pull their wives up to dance. The **SHERIFF** *stands alone, watching.* **MISS LILLIAN** *stares at them all, then runs to the edge of the room and kneels down. Perhaps unseen by the rest, crouched on the floor she breathes. Heavy shuddering breaths, apologising to her body.)*

MISS LILLIAN. Sorry. I'm sorry. I'm so sorry.

(The couples dance. **FRANK** *drinks and dances alone. The dancing is square and the wives are bored.* **JAMES** *stands on* **JAYNE**'*s foot.)*

JAYNE. Ouch!

JAMES. Sorry! I'm sorry/

JAYNE. it's fine, it's, here, let me!

*(***JAYNE** *starts to lead.* **JAMES** *is mortified.)*

JAMES. Jayne! What you doin'?!

JAYNE. It's OK, no one's looking!

JAMES. No, *I'm* supposed to be leading/

JAYNE. well I'm just *better* at it is all, look, let me/

JAMES. no Jayne!

JAYNE. Oh does it really matter who's/

JAMES. what's got into you?! You're acting mighty queer!

JAYNE. I just wanna dance! And keep all ten toes intact!

JAMES. Fine!

(**JAMES** *sulks off to the bar leaving* **JAYNE** *alone. She glares at him, then thinks fuck it, and starts dancing alone. The men are surprised by her courage.* **LOU**, *the* **SHERIFF** *and* **SALLY ANN** *watch in awe, smiling.)*

(The world spirals as we jump forward in time.)

Scene Three

(The music builds, influenced by **JAYNE** *somehow. She lets her hair down. The men are shocked, but also quite like it.* **JAYNE** *raises her hands up to the ceiling and dances freely.* **SALLY ANN** *copies, shyly, then really lets go. The men back away, watching in awe. The* **SHERIFF** *dances to himself in the background, enjoying the music.* **JAYNE***'s body finds* **LOU***'s, and the result is fireworks.* **SALLY ANN** *lets her hair down, twirling and twirling, lost in the music.* **JAYNE** *looks up and sees* **JAMES** *cheering her on, she smiles at him.* **JAYNE** *begins to dance for* **JAMES** *with* **LOU***. The men cheer and jeer.* **LOU** *feels the vibe change and realises what* **JAYNE** *is doing. Heartbroken and humiliated* **LOU** *runs to the door. The music stops dead.)*

FRANK. Lucy! Don't you walk out that door now!

LOU. I need some air!

FRANK. Plenty air in here for ya darlin'.

LOU. I'm going out/

FRANK. no you ain't! I'm calling a lock in! You hear me? No one's leaving this party 'til I say so!

LOU. *(Sarcastic.)* OK Frank, sure thing.

*(***LOU** *goes to exit but* **FRANK** *is suddenly there. He pulls the doors shut and locks them.)*

What the hell?!

FRANK. You heard me!

LOU. Lemme go!

GEORGE. Hey! What's the idea Frank?

FRANK. Somethin's strange with these women!

GEORGE. What?

FRANK. Somethin's goin' on here! I can feel it!

(The men panic slightly.)

JOHN. OK Frank/

JAMES. come on now/

JOHN. come sit down/

FRANK. I'm telling you somethin' ain't right here! They ain't acting right!

LOU. Just lemme go/

FRANK. no!

GEORGE. Frank?! Let her go/

FRANK. I'm telling you somethin' ain't right here!

JOHN. OK Frank, come on now big man/

FRANK. no! Ain't no one leaving 'til things feel normal again!

LOU. This is crazy?!

JAMES. Frank, let's just sit down and/

FRANK. no! Ain't no one leaving my saloon!

LOU. You can't do that!

FRANK. Watch me!

*(**FRANK** raises his gun. Everyone stares.)*

SHERIFF. Frank. Put the gun down.

FRANK. Lillian?

*(**MISS LILLIAN** gets up off the floor, tidies her hair, turns to **FRANK**.)*

MISS LILLIAN. Yes honey?

FRANK. Get the Sheriff here a drink.

*(***MISS LILLIAN*** stares at the* **SHERIFF***, horrified.* **FRANK** *checks the gun is loaded.* **MISS LILLIAN** *walks gently to the bar and slowly pours a shot of whiskey. She passes it to the* **SHERIFF***, apologising silently. The* **SHERIFF** *holds the drink.)*

Cheers!

*(***FRANK*** raises the gun. The* **SHERIFF** *drinks.* **MISS LILLIAN** *can't watch.)*

Another.

*(***MISS LILLIAN*** can't move.)*

Lillian?

MISS LILLIAN. .

FRANK. I'm mighty sorry there Sheriff, my wife seems to have forgotten her fucking manners!

*(***FRANK*** shoves past* **MISS LILLIAN** *to get to the bottle. Everyone is shocked. He pours six shots of whiskey on the bar and motions the* **SHERIFF** *to come over. The* **SHERIFF** *downs all six shots. When the last glass is slammed down* **FRANK** *cheers and the music starts again. The men explode into dancing together, the* **SHERIFF** *included. It's macho and animal and ugly.* **MISS LILLIAN** *backs away to a corner, staring at them, and feeling sick.* **FRANK** *leaves the gun on the bar.* **JAYNE** *starts drinking heavily from the bottle.* **LOU** *sulks in the corner, feeling trapped, trying not to look at* **JAYNE***. The dance ends in sweaty laughter and the men collapse onto chairs.)*

(The world spirals as we jump forward in time.)

(Everyone is at least half-cut. **JAYNE** *and the* **SHERIFF** *are definitely drunk.* **JAMES** *checks himself in the mirror and* **JAYNE** *laughs.)*

JAYNE. Well I'll be! Don't think I've ever known you to spend much time in the looking glass honey? In truth I wasn't even sure you knew quite where it was!

SHERIFF. Oh they know! They all know!

JAMES. Ain't nothin' wrong with a man wanting to look his best. Especially when he's this handsome.

JAYNE. Oh! Humble too!

JAMES. Well of course!

SHERIFF. Ha!

JAMES. There is a bit of vanity among us gentlemen, it's true.

JAYNE. Oh! *Gentlemen* now?

SHERIFF. Ha! As if!

JAMES. Gee, ain't I gentle?

JAYNE. Sometimes.

SHERIFF. Oh!

SALLY ANN. I guess a man does wanna look his best.

JAYNE. What'd you know 'bout what a man wants?!

JAMES. Jayne!

SALLY ANN. Well I, I /..

JAYNE. Thought so.

FRANK. You tell us then Jayne. What's a man want?

JAYNE. Fuckin' and feedin'.

(The men laugh.)

SALLY ANN. Jayne!

FRANK. Got that about right!

SALLY ANN. My goodness!

JOHN. Still, her tongues a little loose no?

JAYNE. Nah you're just uptight!

*(**JAYNE** ruffles **JOHN**'s hair and he immediately smooths it down in the mirror.)*

Oh the vanity!

JOHN. Give over!

JAMES. Easy now honey!

JAYNE. When did men become so terribly vain?

SHERIFF. I blame the reward posters myself. Printed and hung up darn everywhere?! All these images of men/

SALLY ANN. bandits! Criminals!

SHERIFF. Bandits and criminals is true, but *men* all the same. Their image, printed in every town. Gets a man wondering/

JAYNE. if he's as ugly as they say he is?

FRANK. Ha!

JOHN. Well, ain't never had to worry 'bout that before.

JAYNE. You might not but your wife has.

SHERIFF. Hah!

FRANK. Haha that's true!

JAMES. Well gee, the cattle don't seem to mind.

FRANK. You sure 'bout that?

JAYNE. They do moo plenty when they see you!

JAMES. That's cus I'm feedin' 'em!

JAYNE. Is it though?

(The **SHERIFF** *and* **JAYNE** *laugh.)*

SHERIFF. Now now, leave the man be! Ain't his fault he's ugly.

(The **SHERIFF** *laughs and sets* **JAYNE** *off again. Then he tries to be sober and serious, and* **JAYNE** *copies.)*

No! No really! No, now, to continue my point here, if I may/

JAYNE. you surely may/

SHERIFF. my point being /.. What was I sayin'?

JAMES. Oh for gods sake!

JAYNE. About reward posters?

SHERIFF. Yes! Yes, *because*, it kinda *does*, get a man to wondering/

JAYNE. what crime he'd commit?!

SHERIFF. No/

FRANK. what his bandit name would be?

SHERIFF. No/

JAMES. what he'd do with all that money?

GEORGE. Get himself some new boots for a start!

JOHN. Not the boots again/

JAMES. gee these boots are just fine!

GEORGE. Sure!

JAMES. They are!

GEORGE. Sure!

SHERIFF. No no no! Gets a man to wondering 'bout his own image!

JOHN. What *his* face would look like/

SHERIFF. yes! If it were printed/

SALLY ANN. on a *reward* poster?! Heaven forbid!

SHERIFF. I'm just sayin'!

SALLY ANN. Saying *what* Sheriff?

SHERIFF. Well, just that, at least then/

LOU. he's a somebody.

SHERIFF. Yes! Exactly/

SALLY ANN. he's a criminal!

SHERIFF. Yes! And/

SHERIFF, JAMES & JOHN. *everybody* knows it!

JAYNE. That's it? You wanna be known?

JAMES. No. Yeah. Sometimes. It's just /.. I mean, *look!* There he is/

JAMES & LOU. Wanted.

SALLY ANN. For a crime! He's a criminal!

JOHN. Yeah but he's somebody/

GEORGE. to everybody!

SALLY ANN. You're somebody! You're a husband, *my* husband!

JOHN. Yeah but, that ain't going down in no history books.

FRANK. It should! If you survive it!

(Everyone laughs.)

JOHN. Behave!

SHERIFF. But is it not true? That sometimes, a man gets to wondering, *why* exactly it is that he's here?!

FRANK. Well now/

JOHN. what mark he'll leave on the world, when he dies?

SHERIFF. Yes!

SALLY ANN. Heaven forbid!

JOHN. Well we're all gonna die, honey!

SHERIFF. Exactly! So we might as well live for the moment!

(The **SHERIFF** *launches into a dance. The men are amused momentarily, but then quickly irritated. Something about his flamboyance is unacceptable to them.)*

FRANK. Woah there Sheriff! I think that's more than enough!

SHERIFF. Oh you love it!

FRANK. Not sure that I do.

(The **SHERIFF** *stumbles.)*

LOU. Easy there Sheriff.

JAMES. Yeah you wanna be careful Sheriff. Or people will talk!

JOHN. Yeah! And we all know what they'll be saying!

*(***JAMES** *and* **JOHN** *laugh. The* **SHERIFF** *stops dead.* **LOU** *freezes.)*

JAMES. Ain't that the truth!

(Unseen by the others, the **SHERIFF** *walks to the corner and waltzes slowly alone.* **MISS LILLIAN** *watches him from across the room.)*

It's disgusting! All that /.. Men lying with other men?! I ain't never heard of such foul things. Should arrest the whole lot of/

JAYNE. hey hey hey stop that! Why're you talking like that?!

JAMES. Like what?

JAYNE. Like you got *any* idea about the world, when clearly you ain't got a clue James 'bout much of nothin'!

FRANK. Ha! She's got you there James!

JAMES. I'm just sayin'/

JAYNE. well don't! You don't know nothin', so don't be sayin'/

JAMES. I know it ain't right! It ain't natural!

JAYNE. What, now *love* ain't natural?

(**LOU** *looks at* **JAYNE**.)

JOHN. *Love* ain't got much to do with it!

FRANK. Ha! Yeah! They ain't *loving*, Jayne! That ain't what they're doing, sorry to break it to ya/

JAYNE. I know what they're doing, I ain't green! They're loving the way they want to, and I don't think we can judge that.

JAMES. That's not what/

JAYNE. cus look, the truth is, men and men, women and women, women and men, we been loving on each other forever. And that don't mean nothin' but love. And sometimes a little fun. So why you gotta be categorising how people love?

JAMES. I ain't! *They* are!

JAYNE. Who?

JAMES. Doctors! They done a study. A sex study.

JAYNE. *(Laughs.)* A what?!

JAMES. I'm telling ya! They done a study! And they worked out that some people like to be getting up to all sorts and/

JAYNE. well? What's it to you? Honestly, how's it bothering you/

JAMES. it ain't right!

JAYNE. Says who?!

JOHN. God.

SALLY ANN. It clearly states in the Bible/

JAYNE. oh hush your gums Sally Ann! You and I both know just cus it's written in some book don't make it law/

SALLY ANN. how dare you/

JAYNE. not even the gospels are gospel!

GEORGE. Haha that's funny!

JOHN. It ain't.

JAYNE. Ah look, I'm sorry I ain't meaning to be disrespectful about your faith there John, Sally Ann, I really ain't. You believe what you wanna believe/

JOHN. I will/

JAYNE. I'm just saying, it don't feel right to be judging things what ain't hurting nobody!

JOHN. It's the law! They don't just make laws for the fun of it!

GEORGE. Don't they?

JAYNE. Exactly! Seems like they do all the time!

SALLY ANN. Oh don't be so foolish Jayne!

JAYNE. You're the fool Sally Ann! Claim to be Christian and spend all your time judging and hating on people?

SALLY ANN. I will *not* tolerate abuse from you!

JAYNE. Abuse? Oh I ain't even getting started!

JAMES. Jayne?!

JOHN. Stop now, Jayne, you're drunk/

JAYNE. who's rules you living by John?

SALLY ANN. God's/

JOHN. my own!

JAYNE. You sure 'bout that?

JOHN. Of course/

SALLY ANN. what are you/

JAYNE. cus I reckon that'd be worth checking/

JAMES. Jayne/

JAYNE. seems we spend our whole lives living by a set of rules. So I reckon it'd be worth checking that we actually agree with 'em. Cus it's *your* life, right?

JOHN. Right.

JAYNE. And you got your own mind?

JOHN. Sure do.

JAYNE. Good. So use it.

*(**JOHN** and **JAYNE** stare at each other. **SALLY ANN** is in tears again.)*

FRANK. Well now, young Jayne, I think that's plenty outta you!

JAYNE. Oh do ya?

SALLY ANN. Yes!

JAMES. Jayne honey, you're drunk/

JAYNE. so what? So what?!

FRANK. We don't need no radical talk in this here saloon.

SALLY ANN. No!

JAYNE. No only bullshit talk 'bout bullshit laws what don't make no bullshit sense?

JAMES. Jayne! What's got into you?!

JAYNE. Oh JAMES! STOP *SQUASHING ME!*

JAMES. What? I'm not squash/

JAYNE. yes you *are!* I can barely *breathe!*

JAMES. Well, OK?! Hell! I'm just trying my best to love you, but OK/

JAYNE. oh for *god's sake!*

JAMES. What/

JAYNE. don't *sulk!*

JAMES. Well I can't seem to get nothin' right/

JAYNE. then *stop, trying!*

(**JAMES** *looks around, dazed.)*

JAMES. Well hell! I just clear don't understand. You used to be so *sweet* on me Miss Jayne? What's changed?

(At the same time.)

JAYNE.	**LOU.**
Everything!	Nothing!

JAYNE & JAMES. What?!

LOU. Nothing's changed. She's just as selfish as she always was.

JAYNE. Excuse me?!

JAMES. Yeah, what's it gotta do with/

LOU. she does *whatever* she wants!

JAYNE. No I don't!

LOU. Whenever she wants!

JAYNE. No, I/

LOU. hurting people who love her.

*(***JAYNE** *&* **GEORGE** *stare at* **LOU. JAMES** *is baffled.* **LOU** *looks at the floor then at* **GEORGE.***)*

FRANK. Well now, I dunno what on earth is going on?!

JOHN. Me neither!

FRANK. But something's got you all acting mighty queer?!

JAYNE. I'm just being honest! I'm the *only* one who's/

FRANK. OK OK! Why don't you just settle down a little, Miss Jayne.

JOHN. Yeah maybe drink some water!

FRANK. Hah exactly! And let's stop all this nonsense talk now! Ain't no need for you ladies to be worrying 'bout big ole worldly things. We'll take care of all that.

LOU. That what you doing Frank? Taking care of us?

FRANK. Well, what else would I be doing?!

LOU. I dunno. Just seems like you're the only one who gets a say/

JAYNE. exactly!

JOHN. Well now! This is all getting pretty messy!

SHERIFF. Whole country's a mess!

FRANK. Oh don't *you* start/

SHERIFF. a goddamn mess!

JOHN. Sure Sheriff, and you moaning about it is *really* helping!

SHERIFF. Well what are you doing to help eh?

SALLY ANN. He's doing plenty!

LOU. That right?

SALLY ANN. That's right!

JOHN. Thank you honey.

SALLY ANN. He's a good man, living on good principles.

JAYNE. Principles my arse!

SALLY ANN. I'm ignoring you Miss Jayne!

JAYNE. Oh are ya?!

SALLY ANN. I'm rising above it!

LOU. Well mind your head/

JAYNE. haha/

SALLY ANN. to support my husband!

JOHN. Thank you honey!

JAMES. Sheriff's right/

SHERIFF. I often am/

JAMES. whole country is a mess! Got the goddamn Indians charging all over the place/

JAYNE. hey! I told you/

JAMES. Disgusting, barbaric, ignorant/

LOU & JAYNE. no they're not!

LOU. Who told you that?!

JAMES. You don't understand!

JAYNE. How could you be so stupid?!

JAMES. Oh so now I'm *stupid?!*

FRANK. Woah now! How'd we get to bickering again?!

JAYNE. *(To* **JOHN.***)* What *you* been telling him?!

JOHN. *(Laughs.)* Nothing!

JAYNE. You been filling his head with all this?

JOHN. *(Snapping.)* Well it's right ain't it?!

SALLY ANN. *(Shocked.)* John?!

JOHN. Honey, them Indians are living so primitive it's frightening. That, Apache Tribe? They don't even *know* that there's *men, and women!* They got 'em swapping and changing and/

LOU. well maybe that's how they do things!

*(***GEORGE** *stares at* **LOU.***)*

Maybe that's, what's *true,* for them and/

JOHN. you see! People think they can change the rules whenever it suits them?!

FRANK. John/

JOHN. make up *new words,* and new ways of doing things just whenever takes their fancy?! Got all these Europeans, and Mexicans, and Blacks and Homosexuals and/

GEORGE. what you sayin'?

JOHN. Just that! I don't care what you are, what you look like or nothin', just so long as you're respecting what's *right!*

FRANK. John!

JAMES. How'd you mean?

JOHN. Good traditional values! Family values! Christian!

FRANK. John/

JOHN. I'm just saying there's a *right* way to do things!

GEORGE. *(Gently.)* You mean a white way.

*(**GEORGE** stands. Unseen by the others his body starts moving, a subtle dance that grows into a beautiful solo. He transcends above the conversation to somewhere beautiful.)*

FRANK. Woah there! Now that's enough/

JOHN. easy now cowboy/

FRANK. you know my rules! In *this* saloon, there's no guns/

FRANK & JOHN. no politics!

SHERIFF. Except there's always both.

FRANK. Not here, *not* here!

JOHN. Ain't no place for that kinda talk here!

LOU. Easy for you to say.

*(**LOU** watches **GEORGE** dance.)*

FRANK. You see! That's *exactly* the kind of division I'm tryna avoid! That we're tryna escape from, that's why we built this town in the first place!

JOHN. Yeah! Come on now! We're a *family!*

JAMES. Are we?

*(**JAMES** watches **GEORGE** dance.)*

JOHN. Yes!

FRANK. Yes! In *this* town we are! In *this* town/

*(Everyone has suddenly noticed **GEORGE** dancing. It's beautiful and haunting. Searching for release from his own body. **LOU** joins in with the dance. Then **JAMES** joins*

in. Everyone else stares, white with shock. **FRANK** *suddenly can't handle it.)*

NOT *HERE* GODDAMMIT!

(Sudden stillness. Thick silence. Then **MISS LILLIAN** *stands.)*

MISS LILLIAN. They're right!

FRANK. What?!

MISS LILLIAN. You can't ignore it Frank. You can't just pick and choose what you/

FRANK. you don't know *anything*, about, *anything*/

MISS LILLIAN. I know plenty/

FRANK. so I'd suggest you shut your hole!

JOHN. Frank?! Come on now! That's no way to talk to your/

FRANK. get your hands off me!

(Everyone explodes into arguments. Suddenly someone bangs on the door. Everyone freezes. **FRANK** *grabs his gun from the bar.)*

Scene Four

FRANK. Who's there?! We're all armed, and ain't none of us shy. State your name and purpose.

CHARLEY. Charley Parkhurst, aka/

FRANK. One-Eyed-Charley!

EVERYONE EXCEPT CHARLEY. One-Eyed-Charley!

CHARLEY. Ah, so you know my name! Let me in for a drink and I'll share my purpose.

JAMES. *(Loud whisper.)* One-Eyed-Charley! *The* One-Eyed-Charlie?!

SALLY ANN. Oh my god oh my god oh my god/

JOHN. *(Loud whisper.)* quiet woman!

JAMES. *(Loud whisper.)* Gee we gotta let him in!

JAYNE. *(Loud whisper.)* What? No!

JAMES. *(Loud whisper.)* He's a legend! He'll have the most amazing tales to tell us/

JOHN. *(Loud whisper.)* forget the tales! He'll shoot us all dead if we don't/

SALLY ANN. oh my god oh my god oh my god/

FRANK. *(Loud whisper.)* OK OK! *(Calls through the door.)* Come on in Charley!

> *(***FRANK** *unlocks the door. He steps back, still holding the gun. There's a pause then* **CHARLEY** *enters. They're all a bit confused by* **CHARLEY***'s gender.* **CHARLEY** *is used to this.)*

CHARLEY. Howdie boys.

FRANK. Well I'll be damned.

I'm Frank Johnson, I own this here saloon. We got two rules: no politics, no guns

CHARLEY. Good rules.

FRANK. I'll lower mine just as soon as you leave yours in the basket there.

CHARLEY. I will, just as soon as he does.

*(**CHARLEY** nods to **JAMES**, who blushes.)*

And I suspect him too.

*(**CHARLEY** nods to **JOHN**. **FRANK** nods and the men put their guns on the bar. **CHARLEY** puts his two in the basket.)*

FRANK. What can I get ya Charley?

CHARLEY. Whiskey, and plenty of it.

FRANK. Comin' up!

*(**FRANK** pours them all a drink. Everyone stares at **CHARLEY**, who looks around the saloon enjoying the attention.)*

So, what brings you all the way out to these here parts? If you don't mind me asking?

CHARLEY. Ah it's no secret. Pretty common knowledge that I'm chasing that villain Jack Cannon.

FRANK. Who's that now?

CHARLEY. Hell! Could it be possible a man don't know him?!

Well sirs, I'll educate you. This here Jack Cannon, he's a bandit. Goes without saying that he's a good gun. Some say he's the slickest/

JAYNE. gun slinger in The West.

SALLY ANN. Jayne!

CHARLEY. Oh! So you do know him?

MISS LILLIAN. We heard some rumours is all. Foolish bar talk.

CHARLEY. Well now, pretty lady, why don't you tell me exactly what it is you heard/

FRANK. oh I doubt she'd know anythin' you'd wanna hear/

CHARLEY. I doubt she enjoys you speaking for her. Forgive him ma'am, us lads can be overbearing at times. I'd blame it on biology, but in truth it's just plain ole rudeness. Please, proceed.

MISS LILLIAN. It was nothin', just rumours. Never do pay 'em much mind.

CHARLEY. Smart woman.

FRANK. Oh she is. That's why I married her.

CHARLEY. Lucky man.

FRANK. The luckiest.

CHARLEY. And you ain't seen him?

MISS LILLIAN. No sir.

CHARLEY. Yet you know of him.

JAYNE. There was some posters up. A while ago.

FRANK. That right?

CHARLEY. Sure is, I got one right here.

(**CHARLEY** *lays a poster out on the bar. The men glance at it.)*

Hard to believe his brother gone and got himself killed. When our Jack is meant to be such a 'good gun' and all. Don't sound that good to me. So I guess you could say I fancy my chances with the fella, just as soon as I set my sights on him. Say, you ain't seen him have ya?

FRANK. Can't say I have. That the reward price?

CHARLEY. Oh it's double that now.

FRANK. That so?

CHARLEY. Half the country's after him. Got all the best known bounty hunters hot on his heels. That and the law.

(**CHARLEY** *looks at the* **SHERIFF** *who smiles curtly.)*

FRANK. Oh you ain't gotta worry 'bout him.

(The men chuckle.)

He's useless. Ain't that right Sheriff?!

SHERIFF. .

FRANK. So everyone who's anyone's after this Jack fella?

CHARLEY. Pretty much. And especially on account of that little raid he done with the infamous Tommy and those toothless chaps.

FRANK. .

CHARLEY. Gee you ain't heard 'bout that neither?! Jack raided a stage coach with Tommy and his gang. Got his brother killed and Jack escaped with the loot. Now Tommy's after him for revenge and everyone else is after him for the prize. Got the Governor himself chasing him down/

SHERIFF. goddam dirty confederate!

(**CHARLEY** *looks at the* **SHERIFF** *amused.)*

CHARLEY. Gee! A real life Yankee. How original.

FRANK. No politics/

CHARLEY. no guns, I remember. Well anyways, it's true young Jack sure has caused quite a stink.

FRANK. Sounds it.

CHARLEY. Even more so now Tommy put out that warning.

SALLY ANN. What warning?

CHARLEY. Well ma'am. Any town that harbours Jack Cannon gets burned right to the ground.

SALLY ANN. Oh my!

CHARLEY. Oh my indeed.

JAYNE. He ain't been here.

CHARLEY. Well that's good, that's real good ma'am. Cus the good people of Creed let him walk their streets. And now they ain't got no streets. Or people for that matter.

(**CHARLEY** *laughs. No one else does.)*

Anyways, I got a bullet here with his name on it. But before that, I'm all kinds of thirsty.

*(***FRANK** *pours* **CHARLEY** *another shot.* **CHARLEY** *downs it.* **JAMES** *is staring at* **CHARLEY** *like they're the most amazing thing he's ever seen.)*

Somethin' caught your eye?

JAMES. No! I /.. Well, you're Charley Parkhurst.

CHARLEY. All day long.

JAMES. What's it like? Being you?

CHARLEY. Honestly? Fucking great.

(**CHARLEY** *dances and laughs to themselves. Everyone stares.)*

Say, you're all mighty quiet! Like a morgue in here!

FRANK. We ain't used to no visitors is all. Sleepy little town this, a good town.

CHARLEY. Yeah?

JAMES. Yeah. We like things plain and simple.

CHARLEY. Sounds fine to me. *(Looks at* **JAYNE.***)* Mighty fine.

*(***JAYNE** *blushes.* **JAMES** *bristles.* **CHARLEY** *smiles.)*

Not the kinda place you'd invite bandits to.

FRANK. No sir.

CHARLEY. No sir-ee. Especially not the likes of Jack Cannon. Why he's a monster truth be told.

FRANK. That right?

CHARLEY. Oh he seems just fine on the surface. Quite the gentleman. A good gun, good talker, good lookin'. Charm the skirts off any good lady, married or not.

*(***MISS LILLIAN** *bristles.* **CHARLEY** *sees.)*

He's smart, you see? Real good with words. Says all the right things to make a lady feel real special.

JAMES. Wish he'd teach me!

GEORGE. Some men can't be taught.

JAMES. Shuttup!

CHARLEY. Did I mention his music? Oh! He's a mighty fine musician, and it has this wicked effect on women. Oh my, they just go crazy for him! Start moving in new ways. Bodies start making all these shapes they ain't never made.

(The women blush. **CHARLEY** *smiles.)*

FRANK. We'd better learn to sing, hey lads?!

JAMES. And dance too?

JOHN. Good luck!

(The men laugh.)

FRANK. This Jack fella sure sounds like a catch!

CHARLEY. Oh he's the one catching. One woman at a time. *(To* **MISS LILLIAN.***)* Crashing into their lives. Wooing, seducing, screwing. The silly little bitches always melt for him. Open their hearts, open their legs. He fucks 'em, and moves onto the next/

MISS LILLIAN. that's not true!

CHARLEY. Oh dear oh dear! Don't tell me you're another one of Jack's silly little bitches?!

*(***MISS LILLIAN** *suddenly stands.* **CHARLEY** *sees the bump and fake gasps.)*

Well now! *(To* **FRANK.***)* How long did you say you been away?

(Silence. No one breathes. **FRANK** *stares at* **MISS LILLIAN***, slowly stands, and walks towards her.)*

FRANK. Say it ain't true.

MISS LILLIAN. .

FRANK. Just say it's mine.

MISS LILLIAN. .

FRANK. You dirty bitch!

*(***FRANK** *strangles* **MISS LILLIAN.** *No one does anything, frozen with fear.* **MISS LILLIAN** *manages to grab the gun on the bar behind her. She shoots* **FRANK** *in the belly. He falls to his knees. She stares at him.)*

I /.. I was trying, my best, I /..

(**FRANK** *dies.* **MISS LILLIAN** *stares and shakes.* **CHARLEY** *laughs manically.)*

CHARLEY. Well I'll be! You sure got him honey! Straight in the guts! Pow! Yeehah!

SHERIFF. Shut up!

CHARLEY. Yeehah!

SHERIFF. Shut up I say! Lillian, give me the gun.

CHARLEY. Careful there Sheriff, she'll shoot you n all!

SHERIFF. Lillian?

CHARLEY. Can't blame her, to be honest/

SHERIFF. shut up! Lillian, give me the gun.

CHARLEY. All the shit women go through?

SHERIFF. Lillian?

CHARLEY. Hell, I'm surprised they ain't all shooting their husbands!

MISS LILLIAN. Oh my god. Oh my god?! Oh! Oh I /.. Jack? Jack?! JACK?!

(**JACK** *suddenly appears in the doorway.* **CHARLEY** *spins. They stare at each other. They nod. They slowly walk into position. Everyone else gets out of the way.* **CHARLEY** *and* **JACK** *stare at each other, their hands hovering above their gun belts. Silence and stillness.* **CHARLEY** *smiles. They both suddenly draw, BANG! Both spin backwards into the air and crash to the floor. Silence.)*

Scene Five

MISS LILLIAN. Jack?!

*(**JACK** raises a shaky thumbs up and **MISS LILLIAN** runs to them.)*

Oh thank god!

JACK. Lillian, the baby?!

MISS LILLIAN. I'm fine, we're fine! Jack I'm sorry, I'm so sorry/

JACK. I know/

MISS LILLIAN. I just panicked and/

JACK. I know! It's OK/

MISS LILLIAN. It's not! It's not OK/

JACK. I never expected you to chose me/

JOHN. What the hells going on here?!

MISS LILLIAN. What?! Of course I chose you!

JAMES. That's Jack Cannon?!

GEORGE. What?!

JAMES. That's *Jack Cannon!*

*(The men grab their guns and point them at **JACK. JACK** raises their hands. **MISS LILLIAN** stands in front of him.)*

SHERIFF. Woah woah woah!

MISS LILLIAN. Stop!

SHERIFF. Don't shoot!

JOHN. Sheriff?!

GEORGE. What's happening?

JOHN. What the hell's going on here?!

SHERIFF. Don't shoot!

GEORGE. What's happening?!

(**JAYNE** *runs to stand next to* **MISS LILLIAN.**)

JAMES. Jayne!

JAYNE. Don't shoot!

JAMES. Don't shoot!

SALLY ANN. Oh my god!

GEORGE. Step *aside* Jayne!

JOHN. You'll get yourself *killed!*

LOU. No!

(**LOU** *runs to stand next to* **JAYNE.**)

GEORGE. Lucy, no!

SHERIFF. Woah now! Just slow it down fellas/

JOHN. hell's going on here?!

(**MARY** *and* **KID** *run in. The men spin to point their guns at them.*)

JACK, SHERIFF & MISS LILLIAN. No!

SALLY ANN. Oh my god!

MISS LILLIAN. Mary!

SHERIFF. Easy now! Listen up! Everyone lower their weapons/

JOHN. hell is *happening* here?!

SHERIFF. I can explain! But first lower your weapons!

MARY. Ain't no time for that! Jack, they're here! We saw horses on the horizon.

KID. *Big* dust cloud!

MARY. They must be coming in fast!

JACK. How many?

MARY. 'bout a hundred.

SALLY ANN. A *hundred?!*

JACK. How long?

MARY. Minutes! Hell, I'm surprised we ain't dead already!

JACK. Right. This is what you do, take my horse, take Lillian, ride up/

MISS LILLIAN. no/

JACK. to the hills, ride as fast as you/

MISS LILLIAN. no!

JACK. If you stay you'll be killed. If you leave now you might just make it.

SHERIFF. Jack/

MISS LILLIAN. I'm not leaving you!

JACK. Think of the baby!

MISS LILLIAN. I'm *not* leaving you!

SHERIFF. Jack/

JACK. I'll stay and hold them off for as long as I can.

MISS LILLIAN. No!

JACK. This is *my* fault! I caused it, so I gotta fix it.

SHERIFF. Jack/

JACK. go now! While you still/

MISS LILLIAN. I'm not fucking leaving!

JACK. .

MARY. Well if she ain't, I ain't.

SALLY ANN. Mary!

JACK. Take my horse, take Kid, head for the hills/

MARY. and be killed out there?! I'd rather die at home.

JACK. Mary, please/

MARY. I'd rather die fighting than running!

JACK. Then send Kid out!

KID. No!

MARY. He's staying with me.

JOHN. Can someone please explain what's happening?!

JAYNE. Men are coming to kill Jack.

SHERIFF. Not just any men. But Tommy and his gang.

JOHN. So let 'em!

SALLY ANN. John!

JOHN. He ain't nothing to do with us! Let 'em have him/

SHERIFF. Jack's everything to do with us!

JOHN. Have you lost your mind?!

MARY. Even if he weren't it don't matter! Tommy don't exactly fight clean.

SHERIFF. All that we've built here, together?

MARY. They'll take one look at us, and burn us to the ground.

GEORGE. *(To* **JACK.***)* You're bringing them here?

MISS LILLIAN. They're chasing Jack, yes/

GEORGE. you're bringing trouble, to *my* home?!

JACK. Yes. And if you leave now/

GEORGE & JOHN. right, out you go

MISS LILLIAN. No!

JOHN. You've got to go!

LOU & JAYNE. no!

JAMES. We've got to hand him in, or they'll kill us/

KID. they'll kill us anyway! You heard what Charley said!

(Everyone stares at **KID. MARY** *is stunned.)*

We've gotta fight!

*(***KID** *looks to* **MARY***, who has never felt more proud.)*

MARY. He's right!

JAMES. Are you crazy?!

MARY. Might be. But I ain't never had somethin' to fight for 'til now!

JAYNE. Same! There is *nowhere* else I am meant to be but *right* here!

LOU. Same! I can't go back to how I was before.

*(***JAYNE** *holds* **LOU***'s hand.* **JAMES** *stares.)*

JAMES. Jayne?!

SHERIFF. Come on lads! We're running out of time!

GEORGE. Where's the rest of the guns at?!

SHERIFF. Good man!

JAMES. George?! What in the hell you doing?!

GEORGE. Don't look like we got plenty of options?

JAMES. Turn him in! Take the reward money and/

SHERIFF. they'll kill us anyway!

SALLY ANN. Oh god!

MARY. Either way we gotta fight!

JOHN. They're right.

JAMES & SALLY ANN. John?!

JOHN. We have to!

JAMES. This is crazy?!

GEORGE. This is *my* town! My home, my wife /.. Even if she's, if we /..

JACK. We have to work together.

MISS LILLIAN. Yes! Fight together!

SHERIFF. Jack's a good gun, you never know we might just make it.

GEORGE. We won't.

LOU. George!

GEORGE. We won't! But look, we all end up in the dirt anyways. Might as well go out all guns blazing.

MARY. Literally!

GEORGE. This is *our* town. We built it/

JAMES. we'll be *killed!*

MARY. Maybe.

GEORGE. Probably. But I'd say *this,* is somethin' worth dying for.

*(**JAMES** hesitates, then nods.)*

SALLY ANN. Oh god!

JOHN. Come on honey! We can do this!

SALLY ANN. Blessed be the Lord, my rock, who trains/

JOHN. my hands for war/

JOHN & SALLY ANN. amen!

*(**JOHN & SALLY ANN** kiss.)*

LOU. *(To **JAYNE**.)* You in?

JAYNE. Oh I'm all in! I love you!

LOU. I love you!

*(**JAYNE** and **LOU** kiss. **GEORGE** is stunned. **JAMES** is heartbroken.)*

JAMES. Jayne?! What the hell?!

SHERIFF. Plenty of time for that later! Jack?!

JACK. Guns – what we got?

SHERIFF. One rifle, one pistol.

JOHN. Same.

LOU. I've got a pistol/

GEORGE. and a shotgun.

JAMES. Jayne?!

JAYNE. *Later* James!

SALLY ANN. Are we really doing this?!

JOHN, JAYNE, MARY & MISS LILLIAN. Yes!

LOU. Yes! Let's fight!

KID. Fight for love?

MARY. A love worth dying for.

(They group hug. Then armour the fuck up.)

Kid. You stay close to me.

KID. Yes mama.

MISS LILLIAN. Jack, if we get through this alive/

MARY. which we probably won't/

MISS LILLIAN. will you marry me?

MARY & JACK. What?!

SHERIFF. Jack! They're coming!

MISS LILLIAN. Will you?

SHERIFF. Jack?! Quickly!

MARY & MISS LILLIAN. Will you?!

JACK. Yes!

LOU. And you Jayne, will you marry me?

JAMES. *What?!*

SHERIFF. They're coming!

JAYNE. Yes!

JAMES. The *fuck?!*

GEORGE. Lucy?!

SHERIFF. They're here!

JACK. Hide, quickly! Everybody stay low! Don't shoot, until I shout!

ACT THREE

Shootout

(The sound of horses approaching. It's violent and frightening. **JACK** *and the gang huddle together in the middle of the saloon with as many guns as they could find.* **JACK** *points to various areas for them to cover and they split up, pointing their guns out of the windows and cracks in the wooden shutters. The awful noise outside reaches its peak then suddenly stops. Horrible silence.* **TOMMY** *shouts from outside the saloon.)*

TOMMY. Jack? I know you're in there! Come on out now!

*(**JACK** signals for everyone to stay silent.)*

Jack! Don't play games with me! You know how the boys get all kinds of restless.

(The **TOMMY BOYS** *laugh.)*

Jack!

JAYNE. He ain't here!

MISS LILLIAN. *(Hissed.)* Jayne!

TOMMY. Oh don't be foolish now ladies! I know he's there. I know you been hiding him. And look, I'm not angry, I'm just disappointed.

*(**TOMMY** and his **BOYS** laugh.)*

Drop your weapons and come out, or we're coming in! And trust me, you do *not* want these boys coming in!

(The **TOMMY BOYS** *laugh horribly.)*

TOMMY BOY ONE. Yeah! You don't want us coming in!

TOMMY BOY TWO. Pretty bitches!

(The wives raise their guns. **TOMMY** *laughs.)*

TOMMY. Well now! I'm giving you liberated ladies one last chance!

TOMMY BOY ONE. Yeah! You pretty bitches better come out here!

TOMMY BOY TWO. Yeah! Listen up ladies! Or I'm gonna/

*(***LOU** *suddenly stands and shoots out the window.)*

LOU. I ain't no lady.

(Bang bang bang! **LOU** *dives for cover. Windows smash as bullets fly. Everyone is shooting at everyone. It's chaos. Then sudden quiet and stillness.)*

JACK. Everyone OK?!

(Everyone replies.)

SALLY ANN. Oh my god! Oh my god!

JOHN. You're OK honey!

SALLY ANN. *(Struggling with her gun.)* I can't do this!

JOHN. You can!

MISS LILLIAN. Jack? There's too many of them?!

JACK. OK let's split up. Work in pairs. George and James you take the front. John and Sally Ann you take the back. Lillian, come with me. Mary, you cover the side windows with Kid. Sheriff you take the other side. Jayne and Lou, you stay here. OK? Go, go!

(Everyone runs off to their positions. **LOU** *and* **JAYNE** *run to crouch behind furniture, on opposite sides of the saloon. Sudden silence. They look across to each other.)*

JAYNE. Fuck!

LOU. Fuck!

*(***LOU** *and* **JAYNE** *crouch with their guns, waiting for something to happen. Suddenly there's a masked* **TOMMY BOY** *with a gun on the balcony.* **JAYNE** *silently and frantically gestures to* **LOU** *to shoot them.* **LOU** *hesitates, takes a deep breath, and cocks their gun. The* **TOMMY BOY** *hears it and shoots at* **LOU. LOU** *shoots back.* **JAYNE** *cowers as shots are fired back and forth.* **LOU** *keeps standing to shoot then crouching again as their dress is really annoying.)*

Goddamn petticoats!

*(***LOU** *finally manages to shoot the* **TOMMY BOY. LOU** *is shocked.)*

Oh my god?!

JAYNE. Well done!

*(***JAYNE** *crouch-runs over to* **LOU** *and they take cover.)*

You were wonderful!

(They kiss.)

LOU. Get this off me!

*(**LOU** rips off their dress to fight in their under garments. **JAYNE** rips hers off too in solidarity. **MARY** suddenly runs in with a gun in one hand and **KID** in the other.)*

MARY. Oh god it's you!

JAYNE. Mary!

MARY. Jack says to check the Sheriff, but I've got Kid with me.

KID. I'll shoot them! I'll shoot all the bad guys!

*(**KID** shoots his wooden gun. **MARY** looks exhausted.)*

LOU. We'll go. You stay here.

*(**JAYNE** and **LOU** creep off upstage.)*

MARY. Ok Kid, you stay with me now. We need to find somewhere to hide.

KID. I know a place!

*(**KID** takes **MARY** by the hand and pulls her behind the piano. **MARY** is shocked.)*

MARY. You're brilliant!

KID. I know.

*(Gun shots offstage makes them hide. **MISS LILLIAN** runs in, shooting behind her. **MISS LILLIAN** crouches next to **MARY** and **KID. MARY** and **MISS LILLIAN** shoot at the doorway **MISS LILLIAN** just ran through. **KID** shoots their wooden gun. **MARY** keeps pulling him back behind the furniture.)*

MARY. Well this is fun!

MISS LILLIAN. Ha! The most!

*(**MARY** shoots three shots. **MISS LILLIAN** stares at her friend in awe.)*

You're awesome!

MARY. I feel awesome!

MISS LILLIAN. I love you Mary!

MARY. I love you!

(They both simultaneously shoot a man we hadn't even seen. They stand together, guns smoking, looking fucking cool.)

OK, let's move.

*(They crouch-run off, dragging **KID** with them. **JOHN** and **SALLY ANN** appear.)*

SALLY ANN. I can't do it!

JOHN. Yes you can!

SALLY ANN. I can't! I don't even *want* to!

JOHN. We *have* to honey!

SALLY ANN. I won't! I refuse!

JOHN. Well fine! We'll all just be shot then!

SALLY ANN. Well good!

JOHN. Good!

*(The **SHERIFF** appears, in a glittery dress, with a shotgun. He crouches next to **JOHN**.)*

SHERIFF. John.

JOHN. Sheriff.

SALLY ANN. .

JOHN. Nice frock.

SHERIFF. Thanks!

JOHN. Going out in style?

SHERIFF. Something like that.

(They shoot together. **SALLY ANN** *cowers. Elsewhere we see* **JAMES** *and* **JAYNE** *shooting together at a* **TOMMY BOY** *across the space.)*

JAMES. WHAT THE FUCK JAYNE?!

JAYNE. NOW'S REALLY NOT THE TIME!

JAMES. YOU'VE BROKEN MY HEART!

JAYNE. I'M SORRY!

JAMES. I THOUGHT YOU LOVED ME?!

JAYNE. YEAH, WELL, I THOUGHT A LOT OF THINGS!

JAMES. I THOUGHT WE WERE HAPPY?!

JAYNE. NO! WE WERE ASLEEP!

JAMES. WHAT?

JAYNE. AND NOW I'M AWAKE!

*(***JAYNE** *shoots a man over* **JAMES** *shoulder. He's shocked she saved him.)*

JAMES. WHAT HAS *HAPPENED* TO YOU?!

JAYNE. I DON'T KNOW! BUT AIN'T IT MARVELLOUS?!

(The gun fight continues. More **TOMMY BOYS** *appear. Our gang suddenly look outnumbered.)*

JAMES. Fuck!

SHERIFF. Steady lads!

JOHN. Oh sweet Jesus!

*(***JACK** *suddenly appears and looking like an absolute rock star, kills all the* **TOMMY BOYS** *in one smooth combination.)*

JAMES. Wow!

JACK. James, cover that window. Jayne, you take that one. Where's George?

(**GEORGE** *suddenly appears.)*

GEORGE. Here!

JACK. Cover that side!

GEORGE. Got it!

(**LOU** *suddenly appears.)*

JACK. Lou, you're with George.

LOU. Right.

JACK. John, Sally Ann, you take the front porch. Sheriff, Lillian you're with me.

SHERIFF. Yes sir.

(**JACK** *exits with the* **SHERIFF**. *Everyone moves to their positions. Silence.)*

JAMES. *(Hissed.)* I can't believe you'd do this to me!

JAYNE. *(Hissed.)* Not *now* James!

JAMES. *(Hissed.)* We're childhood sweethearts! We're destined to be married!

JAYNE. *(Hissed.)* Not anymore.

JAMES. *(Hissed.)* Are you honestly choosing *her* over me?

JAYNE. *(Hissed.)* Him.

JAMES. *(Hissed.)* What?

JAYNE. *(Hissed.)* It doesn't matter. I'm not choosing *either* of you! I'm choosing *me!*

JAMES. *(Hissed.)* What?!

(The **TOMMY BOYS** *suddenly appear. Everyone is shooting at everyone over the gun fire.)*

WHAT'S WRONG WITH ME?!

JAYNE. NOTHING! YOU'RE GREAT!

JAMES. IF IT'S SOMETHING I CAN CHANGE?!

JAYNE. NO!!

(Sudden pause in the gunshots.)

James, you're great! You're *really* great! Honestly, you are ticking *all* the boxes. They're just, not *my* boxes.

(Bang bang bang!)

LOU. GOOD SHOT!

JAYNE. THANKS!

(Bang bang bang!)

GEORGE. I JUST DON'T GET IT!

LOU. WHAT'S THERE TO GET?

GEORGE. WHY D'YOU WANNA DRESS LIKE A MAN?

LOU. I DUNNO! MAYBE I AM A MAN?!

(Bang bang bang!)

JAMES. THE WEDDING IS OFF!

JAYNE. GREAT!

JAMES. I SAID IT'S *OFF!*

JAYNE. I SAID *GREAT!*

JAMES. YOU DON'T EVEN CARE?!

(Bang bang bang!)

GEORGE. OK!

LOU. WHAT?

GEORGE. I SAID *OK!*... BEHIND YOU!

*(**GEORGE** kills a man behind **LOU**.)*

LOU. Thank you!

*(**JOHN** sprints in and crouches trying to load his gun, with hands jittery with adrenaline. Silence. **SALLY ANN** tiptoes in, the gun shaking in her hands.)*

SALLY ANN. *(Hissed.)* John? John?!

*(A **TOMMY BOY** suddenly appears and **SALLY ANN** freezes, her hand over her mouth. The **TOMMY BOY** doesn't see her, his eyes set on **JOHN**, who's still trying to reload his gun. The **TOMMY BOY** raises his gun at **JOHN** and cocks it. **JOHN** looks up, terrified. **SALLY ANN** shoots the **TOMMY BOY** dead.)*

Oh my god!

*(**SALLY ANN** is frozen to the spot staring at the gun in her hands. **JOHN** rushes over to her, and pulls her behind the piano for protection.)*

JOHN. Honey! You did it!

SALLY ANN. I, I killed a/

JOHN. you saved me! You saved me honey, saved my life!

SALLY ANN. I love you.

JOHN. I love you!

*(**LOU** bursts in and is shot in the shoulder, spinning in the air before crashing to the*

ground. **JAYNE** *runs in one door.* **JAMES** *runs in another.)*

JAYNE. LOU!

*(***JAYNE** *goes to run to* **LOU**, *but* **JAMES** *signals for her to stop.)*

JAMES. No! Stop STOP!

*(***JAYNE** *hesitates, but thinks fuck it, and runs to* **LOU. JAMES** *sees a* **TOMMY BOY** *aim at* **JAYNE. JAMES** *dives across the saloon, taking the bullet for* **JAYNE. JAMES** *crashes to the ground.* **JAYNE** *spins on the spot, stuck between* **LOU** *and* **JAMES.** *Everyone enters and stares at* **JAMES** *as he dies.)*

JAYNE. James! Oh god!

LOU. Jayne!

*(***JAMES** *dies. Everyone stares, hopeless.* **MISS LILLIAN** *looks around, grabs the shotgun and stands centre stage.)*

MISS LILLIAN. We said we'd fight for love?!

*(***MISS LILLIAN** *fires off a round to the sky. The* **SHERIFF** *runs to the piano and plays. Music kicks off. Everyone line dances with fierce fuck-you faces.)*

SALLY ANN. OH MY GOD! OH MY GOD!

JOHN. YOU'RE DOING GREAT HONEY!

(The gunfight continues. The stage is chaotic. As people crouch-run across the stage with more ammunition, or changing of positions, they sometimes meet in the middle and have a mini dance. It's surreal and brilliant. The dancing becomes more jagged and fractured.

Everyone raves together centre stage. **TOMMY** *suddenly appears and has a knife to* **MISS LILLIAN***'s throat. Everyone scatters.* **JACK** *has a gun pointed at* **TOMMY**. *Silence.)*

TOMMY. Where's the money?

JACK. Let her go!

TOMMY. I won't ask again!

MISS LILLIAN. Jack! Please!

(**JACK** *lowers their guns to the floor and slides them towards* **TOMMY**. *Everyone else stands in a clump hostage.* **JACK** *gets on their knees.* **TOMMY** *pushes* **MISS LILLIAN** *away, and pulls a gun on* **JACK. MISS LILLIAN** *joins the upstage clump.)*

JACK. It's buried. With Harry. Where he died.

TOMMY. How sentimental. You dirty, double-crossing snake. D'you know, I enjoyed shooting your brother. I'll enjoy shooting you more.

(The **SHERIFF** *shoots* **TOMMY**. *Everyone stares at the* **SHERIFF**.*)*

SHERIFF. We won!

*(***TOMMY** *shoots the* **SHERIFF**. *The* **SHERIFF** *dies.* **JACK** *shoots* **TOMMY** *three times.* **TOMMY** *dies. Silence and stillnes.)*

JACK. We won, for now. But there'll be more. There's always more

*(***MISS LILLIAN** *stands next to* **JACK. LOU** *cradles the dead* **SHERIFF**. *Everyone reloads their guns.* **MARY** *starts singing. Everyone slowly joins the song. The dead rise and join the song. They gather and sing together.)*

ABOUT THE AUTHOR

Charlie Josephine is an actor, writer and director. They are passionate about honest sweaty storytelling that centres working class women and queer people. Their acclaimed work for theatre includes *I,Joan* (The Globe 2022); *Bitch Boxer* (Soho Theatre Young Writers Award 2012, Old Vic New Voices Edinburgh Season 2012, British Council Showcase 2013, Holden Street Theatre's Award 2013, Clonmel Theatre Award 2014 and Adelaide Fringe Award 2014); *BLUSH* (Underbelly Untapped Edinburgh Season 2016 and The Stage Edinburgh Award 2016). As an actor, Charlie played 'Mercutio' In Erica Whyman's 2019 RSC touring production of *Romeo and Juliet*. Other acting credits include *Metamorphoses* (The Globe 2021), 'Secret Theatre' (Lyric Hammersmith 2013) and 'Julius Caesar' (Donmar Warehouse 2012). Charlie is an associate artist at the NSDF and a board member at Cardboard Citizens. They are currently under commision at NT Connections and Headlong Theatre. They're also developing a new feature biopic with Salon Pictures.

Milton Keynes UK
Ingram Content Group UK Ltd.
UKHW021843250124
436705UK00010B/217